Ordinary Childhood Dreams

or Simply Psycho

Oliver Raymond Knell

ISBN: 978-1-910115-57-2

This creation is nonfiction but all names have been changed to protect identities.

Dedication

For Dad because he never had the opportunity to understand.

Table of Contents

Prologue

How do you spot the firefighter who has OCD?

He's the one who wipes his feet on his way into the burning building in case he gets the carpets dirty, and organises the baked bean tins in the kitchen cupboard before he leaves.

There are over four hundred conditions registered as sitting within the broad spectrum of mental disorders. Many illnesses such as bipolar disorder, schizophrenia, anorexia nervosa, bulimia nervosa, alcoholism, drug addiction and Alzheimer's are familiar to us in name only.

Mental illness has for many years been something of a dirty expression, forbidden for discussion in polite company, created by centuries of ignorance and fear. The stigma attached to anything other than a bespoke physical illness, and the inability of the masses to understand the power of the brain and the chemical influences that act upon it remain amongst humanity's greatest travesties.

The World Health Organisation has ranked Obsessive-Compulsive Disorder (OCD) in the top ten of the most debilitating illnesses of any kind in terms of loss of earnings and diminished quality of life. My story begins here.

Ordinary Childhood Dreams

The suicidal man lies broken on the bed,
Blood trickles from the wound self-inflicted to his head,
Why did he do it? To hurt his family?
No, to forget the life he hated, at last he could be free.

He understands the pain he's caused for sisters and for others,
He leaves a dying tribute to the hearts and souls of mothers.
They take the hurt but never show the sorrow that he gives,
But he can feel the intense pain, every second that he lives.

The welcome end has come for him as the blood falls to the floor,
The intelligent and faithful son will play a part no more.
But in his soul the love remains, he has saved his family,
Wherever he rests, in heaven or hell, at peace he'll always be.

1974

Writing stuff like this in my early teenage years probably should have activated alarm bells within me or at least for those who were closest to me. Maybe they were aware that I was different but just couldn't quite put their finger on exactly what it was. Perhaps they were too busy, too preoccupied with making ends meet to have the energy or inclination to address any concerns they may have had.

Most of my writing around that time was indicative of a dark and acutely pessimistic world, heavily influenced by a sense of fear and doubt, a product of something that even I didn't understand.

I think my life may have started for real when I was around the age of nine. Well, at least that is what it feels like as I remember very little of the preceding years. Nothing significant anyway, memories erased by the passage of time or just wishful thinking.

I was a rather small child, angel-faced and with what I suppose some would interpret as a sweet and innocent nature. To the outside world I always appeared happy and was often told that my bright blue eyes sparkled as I smiled. The problem for me was that I always felt different, remote from everyone else; almost as if I were looking in from the outside, not quite fitting anywhere. My four sisters all seemed more content, able to chat and play, join in and enjoy their childhood. I don't suppose they were particularly happy but from an observer's perspective it certainly felt like I was missing out in some way.

Whenever I looked in the mirror I could see sadness looking back at me and the more I observed, the more I worried about the future. I wondered if I even had a future. Looking back I am not certain about anything and I regularly question my recollection of events. Memories fade and I guess we seek to reinvent our childhood years with an idealistic view, particularly if childhood was insignificant or unfortunate, but for me I know the past was dark and lonely.

Ordinary Childhood Dreams could make you sad. It may make you cry or encourage you to consider the meaning of life. I simply hope it provides the desire to feel for a lost soul, to understand the power of the human brain and the strength required to defeat the curse of a lifetime. Believe me, it can be beaten.

1. Do I really want to do that?

We went to the seaside one day in the '60s, and had to stop halfway there. Cars were pretty rubbish in those days, well at least our cars always were. Journeys were a total nightmare, sitting in the back of a cramped, smelly old crate; leather seats too old to maintain their dignity and harbouring the residue of years of abuse and neglect.

Sisters, four in total, all squashed up like sardines in a rusty tin. Thank heavens we stopped; contending with all the pinching and poking without Mum and Dad seeing what was going on was becoming a nightmare. Dad would have killed us if he had known. No, he really would have: he was pretty angry sometimes and he scared the shit out of me. I think I still loved him, though. Anyway, I remember feeling pretty fed up that day because that was all it was back then, being fed up, not actually aware at the time of quite how different I was.

We were all released from the confines of our cigarette-smoke-filled prison and told to wipe our snotty noses and tuck ourselves in, make our hair look presentable and walk in an orderly manner to the café. It wasn't going to be a thrilling experience but better than nothing, I supposed.

The facilities looked rather dull and uninviting and I didn't think the cups and cutlery would be very clean; after all, that is very important to a nine-year-old boy, isn't it?

Mum followed behind, making sure that no one did anything that could be considered silly or disrespectful to Dad.

He walked ahead in his usual inimitable style. Arrogantly striding, manfully and in control, with his brood of eager little chicks following behind. Mind you, he was still pretty handsome then, with a strong jaw and imposing physique. Scruffy bastard though. He didn't make much of an effort with his personal hygiene, and he smoked so many Kensitas (which made Woodbines seem like caviar) that he permanently exuded a trail of smoke like a choking 1940's locomotive. When he got angry, part of the fear I felt resulted from his toxic breath that was surely as corrosive as any acid.

The entrance to the café was in sight and all we had to do was to cross a very busy carriageway. I don't think anyone had thought of safety and the idea of a crossing or a footbridge was still a few years away. It was then that I first realised that danger was a real issue and something on which I had a real focus.

No one else seemed to care, but this busy road was a nightmare, something to be feared and given a great deal of respect. The traffic sped by, spewing fumes in my face; the noise was deafening inside my young, inexperienced head and all I could think of was that I wished I was at home, away from any danger or temptation. A large truck approached and I worried that my mum was too close to the roadside; it crossed my mind that the passing vehicle could drag her into its path and crush her under its thundering wheels.

Suddenly, as if it had crept up on me like a slithering snake dealing its killer blow to a poor unsuspecting rabbit, the thought occurred. What if Mum fell under the wheels? What if I should have stopped it happening? What if it was my fault that she was too close to the roadside? What if I somehow bumped into her and her small mousey frame stumbled uncontrollably into the gutter to be removed from my life forever? Oh my God, I thought, what if all of the previous worries were a cover story, because my actual intent was to end Mum's life by giving her a hefty shove into that abyss of rubber and steel. Did I want to kill her?

My brain was working at an earth-shattering speed, panic set in, and I thrust my hands into my pockets to prevent that terrible scenario becoming a reality. The nerve ends jangled as the impulses in my brain tried to influence the action of my muscles. No way could I do it, would I do it. The test of strength had begun, the test that would rule my life for the next forty five years or so.

How could I prove that I didn't want to do such an awful thing? *I know,* I thought, *I will raise my hand and pretend to place it at the critical point where Mum will fall forward and submit to the wheels of a speeding truck.* The hand went back in my pocket. I had proved it: I was not an evil boy at all. The feeling of complete absolution lasted all of sixty seconds as the curse tried to persuade my overactive brain to re-enact the scenario, just to make sure that the evidence stood up.

No, I definitely didn't want to do it. The nightmare had started with a vengeance and this would shape my future as a child, a teenager, a young adult and into the distant future.

We walked into the Greasy Joe café and my stomach turned with a sickness that has become so familiar over the years. The dirty knives and forks were the least of my concerns. This, combined with the almost paralysed feeling in my arms and legs, made the whole experience something that I would always recognise as the onset of a period of decline. 'Peaks and troughs' my first psychiatrist would tell me some eighteen years later when I had a breakdown, a meltdown, an episode or, as I put it at the time, 'I went a bit nutty and had to seek help and protection from myself'.

For as long as I can remember, I have been obsessive and compulsive. Obsessively seeking information, questioning incessantly, always wanting to understand and analyse every small event. Forever looking at all aspects of my life with a fine-tooth comb and eventually discovering that I may as well have accepted the starting position. Why? Because more analysis creates more concerns and subsequently further analysis. This was my circle of life and for a young boy with so much brain space to fill, the scope was endless. I had the capacity to build my automatic responses ad infinitum.

The problem I found with the constant questioning was that everyone in the room, the house and the playground, not forgetting myself, longed for me to shut up and talk about sensible things, to have some fun and live like a child for as long as possible. I don't know why but it seemed normal to me that I should understand everything in order to be a better person and make the right decisions. If I didn't know what the solution was, how could I move forward?

Watching the old black and white television was challenging, because whilst the family would be enjoying the latest edition of *Bonanza* or *The High Chaparral*, I would be wondering why the horse didn't wander off after not being tied securely to the rail outside the saloon. The film that Dad wanted to watch in silence threw up so many anomalies that I could not resist the temptation to ask why, how, who, where and when. My brain was unable to settle on 'just because it is'.

The most frustrating part of all of this is that although everyone got fed up with me, I doubt very much if they got as fed up with me as I did with being me. When the pressure grew too great and the responsible adults could take no more, I would disappear to my bedroom and revisit the problem until it became clear in my head. Repetition seemed to be the answer because finally I would reach a point where the chemicals in my brain would send the message: 'Yes, that's OK, now you can relax', or I would be so tired and worn out from the pressure of my research that my mind and body would succumb to an uneasy sleep.

In some ways the constant searching for answers was a compulsive reaction to my obsessional nature and what I would understand later in life to be a fruitless, unrewarding and damaging waste of my waking and sleeping hours.

There was no end to the cycle and I liken the repetitive nature of the illness to a colony of blind soldier ants that after faithfully following a pheromone trail left by others on a mission, then lose contact with the trail. Should enough of these blind disciples lose the scent, they follow the ant immediately in front. This new movement becomes a continuous spiral that has no end or starting point and the army continues in ever decreasing circles to ultimate death.

I sometimes think of my early obsessional behaviour as that picture of the snake eating its own tail. The iconic ouroboros symbol originates from Ancient Egypt and although I accept it has little to do with OCD, to my mind it often felt like I was searching for my purpose in life whilst eating away at my sanity. I wonder if everyone had known how weird I was, would they have had me committed to the county asylum wearing a back-to-front jacket? Not sure if they took minors in; probably not.

2. A taste of Church of England education.

Nine years old is a difficult age when all you seem to do is use your alleged 'higher than average' intelligence to destroy your enjoyment of life. Yes, Mrs E. M. Davies, head teacher at the village school, reckoned my IQ came out at a similar level to professors and those that follow a path of enlightenment. Emily Mary obviously liked me but then I think she was intrigued by my angelic appearance and complex character.

'Oliver,' she would say in that deep, penetrating, somewhat manly tone, 'You are such a bright boy, but you look so troubled. Is everything OK at home?'

'Yes, Mrs Davies, fine thank you,' I would say, whilst thinking, *Fine if you don't count the rows that Mum and Dad always have, the hours I spend at night going through my bedtime rituals, the tears that roll down my cheeks before sleeping because I cannot understand where the thoughts come from and I don't know who to ask for help.*

Do you think she would have understood? No, of course not: OCD was not 'invented' until years later. She would no doubt have thought, *What a strange little boy you are, Oliver, you do make me smile. You are so bright, but maybe you dwell on things too much.* She didn't have a clue that the rituals and prayers that took me at least half an hour every night had to be done, or else Dad would probably kill Mum and it would be my fault. *My fault!* Yes, of course, because the repeated words would alleviate the pressure in my head and resolve the worries that he was going to harm her, for one night at least. Of course, I didn't know at the time that this was how the compulsions grabbed you, chewed you up and then spat you out with the worries of the world on your shoulders.

There was some realism in the fears I had nurtured, because my parents could hardly be considered the most stable couple on the estate and that really was saying something given the demographics of the community. The neighbours were pleasant enough, I suppose, but at the same time I felt that we didn't really fit in, almost like we were intruding. Moving house at least four times since starting school and attending as many different junior schools failed to provide a comfortable and consistent environment in which to grow and develop. We were, I believe, almost viewed as a transient family and with continually having to make new friends, knowing that they were unlikely to stay in our lives for very long, I suppose I built up a force field around me to avoid further damage.

The harm I thought my Dad could do to Mum was perhaps not particularly realistic as I guess all parents argue, but there was something about the isolation I felt that made me create a means of protecting her just in case, albeit in my mind only. Thinking back now, I cannot believe how troubled I must have been to remember all of those ridiculous sayings and lists, and recite them night after night, absolutely word for word. How could anyone, especially a bright nine-year-old, think that words could protect anyone? That's likely to be the reason I called my evening sessions 'prayers' because all children know that praying means there is always salvation. I am by no means religious and never have been, but this seemed to be the safest option at the time.

The best bit about all of this was that after I had gone through the systematic and gradually more complex ritual dictation on Saturday nights, there was a possibility that a father in an abnormally good mood may give me a shout at 10:00 p.m. and allow me to watch *Match of the Day*. For a football mad youngster that was another good reason to pray for peace and harmony in the household. Don't get me wrong. It didn't often happen but while there was the slightest chance, it was worth a shot.

The big concern for me was that I felt the need to take responsibility for all the bad things that happened in the world; well, those that occurred in my world anyway. If it was worth worrying about it, it was obviously my fault.

My waking hours were completely and mercilessly filled with all sorts of ritualistic behaviour; ruled by counting, washing, praying, crying, self-discussion (talking to myself) and creating a capsule of doom into which no one had authority to enter. It was a huge challenge as only I knew what was going on, but to live in that world whilst appearing normal to all those around me was an extremely difficult act to perfect and one that I would need to develop further as time passed.

Going to school was always a treat because it allowed me to focus on trying to be the cleverest boy in the class. The school consisted of two classes, infants and juniors, and the lessons were not structured to any particular age group or level of intelligence. We all did the same lessons to the same degree of difficulty and it was amazing to think that anyone was able to develop at all. I was lucky because I found the work easy and always wanted to analyse that simplicity to reason why it worked, why it behaved that way and what it all meant. My intrigue was driven by a need to occupy my thought processes fully in order to shut out the nasty fears and feelings that were threatening to overpower me.

It doesn't seem fair that someone of such tender years had the burden of a seemingly endless chain of pain thrust upon them, but who would listen? Who would ease that pain and remove it to where it belonged?

3. Abstract thoughts

Maybe, if I became a professor or a scientist or a spaceman, I would be able to explore the real meaning of life, and to dare to go where no man had gone before. I would be far too busy to worry about stupid thoughts, or to concern myself with my responsibilities as protector of all, and other comparatively insignificant issues. If you had seen me sitting in the classroom wondering how I could escape my living hell, making sure that I recited the right words in the correct order in my head, checking that I hadn't forgotten what I needed to say, do, or how to behave, you may well have sympathised. The innocence, external calm, and quiet confidence that betrayed the real me must have been quite appealing, albeit concealing the evil lying just below the surface. Yes, that is what I was: evil, manipulative, sinister and mean. Those nasty thoughts and feelings were not just invented, they were absolutely real and that reality was numbingly debilitating. No one else felt the way I did, of that I was certain.

During the 1960s and '70s no one seemed to have a clue what I was experiencing and to this day I wonder how I ever survived in a place where I felt so isolated from reality. The same period had seen huge gains in terms of medical advancement in so many areas but it seemed that mental illness had maintained its sinister reputation and had remained an enigma, something that needed to be hidden from plain sight, no questions asked. Medical science had recently delivered the miracle of vital organ transplantation, including heart, lungs, kidneys and liver. Geneticists had dramatically improved their knowledge of DNA, and numerous other remarkable discoveries that paved the way for the replication of life itself were thrust upon humanity. I wonder why, during a period of rampant medical enlightenment, I was left to stagnate in my personal, uncertain world. Perhaps it was my social background, family history, simple ignorance or just the stigma of mental illness itself that created the barriers to diagnosis and treatment. Was my affliction so shameful that no one wanted to ask the right questions, or was it that the right questions would provide unpalatable answers?

They could all see that things were not quite right with me but I guess it would have been very difficult for anyone to put their finger on what was actually wrong. Consequently, for a number of years I tried my hardest to keep things to myself for fear of finger-pointing and potential recrimination. I already felt extremely isolated and didn't wish to increase the risk of being exposed to everyone as a weirdo.

It would have been especially difficult to talk to anyone about the thoughts in the early years; I mean at least until I was old enough to realise that there was something very wrong with the way I felt about things. It's quite scary to think you are different and, as I explained earlier, having moved constantly from place to place during those formative years, the lack of belonging had already made me, and I should imagine the girls too, feel very insecure in our surroundings on so many occasions. Having said that, I must admit I do recall speaking to my mother briefly about my feelings when I was around eleven years old. I had been feeling extremely low as my Dad had been particularly scathing regarding my seeming inability to act like a real boy; you know, the sort that fights and gets his knees dirty and scraped but also helps with fixing the car and knows what each spanner looks like and where to find it in a hurry.

He always had a decrepit car, but in those days cars were simple to work on. I think they only had a carburettor, an alternator, spark plugs and a head or something like that, not forgetting an exhaust pipe and a steering wheel. That was all I knew anyway, after years of 'helping' under duress.

Even Dad was pretty inept at it, but spent most weekends tuning up the already smooth-running old crate. He liked big American cars for some strange reason, the type that when abandoned outside our council house would take up the parking space for three houses. It didn't bother him though, it was just tough luck on the neighbours. I knew immediately on hearing, 'Be doing a bit on the car at the wickend (weekend) so you can help me,' that I was in for trouble. I just didn't get it at all, and all I had to do was to fetch and carry the tools from the asbestos-clad shed and occasionally pump the brake pedal if I was really lucky.

I forever got it wrong, and being overtly obsessional I had started to dread the call, 'Just fetch that three-quarter spanner, Bronco.' Bronco was a name only he tended to call me, despite my hating it throughout childhood. It seems that when I was a baby I constantly bounced up and down in my pram as if I were riding a horse and this reminded him of one of his favourite TV programmes starring a cowboy called Bronco Lane.

Anyway, I had always worked myself into such a state through consistently getting it wrong that I could never find that three-quarter spanner. It could even be sitting right there on the workbench in front of me, ready to jump out at him when he lost his temper and stormed into the shed muttering under his tobacco-charged breath, swearing about this idiot.

Was that inability to find things linked to my OCD? Perhaps not, but the fear it created certainly didn't help if you wanted to talk to your parents about sensitive or potentially earth shattering confessions.

When I finally found the courage to speak to Mum about the weird thoughts I had been having, I told her that I kept thinking horrible things and asked if it meant that I wanted to harm someone. I think I combined the initial enquiry with a question about sexuality and why I had been experiencing strange sensations in my loins for the first time. I surmised that would provide an escape clause in the event that she reeled in shock at the initial enquiry.

I vividly remember being told to speak to Dad about this and the opportunity arose whilst we were on a very rare trip as a family to Longleat Safari Park in Wiltshire. We camped on a field adjacent to the park, and so it was to the background sound of lions roaring in the early evening I walked across the field with an extremely embarrassed man, who at the age of thirty seven had never had to speak to anyone with anything that remotely resembled sensitivity. He had obviously been given a few tips as to what he may be asked but his assumptions were wide of the mark.

He quite rightly advised me that the feelings I was experiencing were normal and that it was good that I could talk to him about such things. Strangely he believed that the other issue, the off-the-wall thoughts about violence and harm, were inextricably linked to the sexual thing in that it was a growing-up experience and quite plainly something I would grow out of in a couple of years.

'But, Dad, it scares me and I don't know why I think stuff like pushing Mum under a car. When I'm on my own with people sometimes I worry that I want to harm them, I know I don't really want to but it keeps going around and around in my head.' I didn't know what depression was at that time and had learned to interpret the feelings of impending doom and utter sadness as normal.

Now I wish I was back in that position, because after years of living with this 'normal' state of mind, I find that during the darkest times the thunder clouds of depression flood my heart and claw at my very soul. They strive to attack any sense of rational reasoning, remove it and replace it with a desire to act on impulse and do exactly the things that are creating the pain in the first place.

Dad was absolutely right: it is normal because when he was a kid he had a feeling that he hated farmers and would have been quite happy if he could have killed all of them. He laughed when he explained that he and his brothers went poaching rabbits and pheasants as early teenagers, and often got rumbled by landowners and farmers. The boys were quick to run away and escape with all manner of ill-gotten gains but back in the day a bit of poaching was just what you did. He had a tough upbringing, having little money or guidance from an absent, alcoholic father and a mother who ruled with a rod of iron, and was completely unfamiliar with the concept of love and kindness.

Well, that little discussion ended with me thinking Dad wanted to kill all farmers, but that was normal in his eyes because they had caught him and his brothers in the act and it served them right. He was keen to add that as payback and to make sure that the rotten sods suffered, he and his brothers would launch roofing slates at the farmers' chickens and if they got lucky, a good shot would decapitate one of them. The boys could enjoy the show as the 'headless chicken' ran around for a while. I honestly don't know if the story was true but after a little research I discovered that the brain doesn't control all body movement and a neural pathway in the spinal cord is pre-programmed in such a way that the muscles are able to continue moving without a brain to guide them. He may have been telling the truth for once.

The chat didn't help. I think after that I decided it would be sensible to avoid discussing my worries with my parents as it was highly likely that the journey to understanding would be fraught with contradictions and a lack of knowledge. But then how could I expect either of them to understand? I wasn't blaming them. They were merely part of a society that not only didn't comprehend the affairs of the brain, but wanted to pretend that mental illness was all in the mind.

4. Kids will be kids.

They were all normal, happy children running around in the playground, giggling and shouting, enjoying the freedom of the age and the warm summer sunshine. They all had happy family lives; loving, caring parents, grandparents that visited at the weekend and provided sweets and hugs. Their mums and dads loved each other and held hands and kissed goodbye in the mornings and embraced each other after just an hour apart. The kids were as poor as us in our humble council house, but they were rich in comparison because they didn't constantly have to face their demons.

They let me play football with them every single day, but I knew that I was never one of the 'inner circle'. That was obvious because when I wanted the ball, they always passed to someone else, and when I scored a goal they failed to understand how important that was. They knew I was good, but forgot to tell me and I needed to be told because inside my head I knew that I would never be quite good enough and if I were to achieve the heady heights of 'good enough', no one would believe it, least of all me.

The boys thought I was effeminate and they called me 'poof boy' and that was probably the nicest thing they ever said. Perhaps my jeans fitted with a bespoke side zip didn't deter the doubters. Why Mum made me wear the girl's hand-me-downs is beyond me.

They still wanted to play football with me because I was obsessed with it and would always go in goal. If I was alone I played 'keepie up' in the garden for hours and hours. Alternatively, I would hammer the old, leather case ball against the wall of the house until I got yelled at by Dad who was trying hard to concentrate on having a go at Mum. I had to be careful to avoid the piles of dog mess in the garden, deposited by our two canine pets. The adults had no impetus to pick it up and dispose of it safely because my weekly grass cutting chore would do the job. So at least once a week the stuff ended up in the mower box, when it didn't get spread more widely that is.

I suspect that this aspect of my young life was the reason for one of my most enduring fears. The damage that could be caused by the stuff that the dogs left behind was clearly not an issue for everyone else. No one seemed to care at all and at the tender age of ten, only I knew that children could lose their life, their sight, or go mad if they were unfortunate enough to tread in this kind of waste matter. You could accidentally get some on your hands and that would be it. Eternally contaminated, the suggested cure is immediate and prolonged washing of hands. My self-imposed instructions for this procedure were as follows:

- Water must reach the required temperature, and for an experienced practitioner, this is simply as hot as possible.
- Hands must be held under this stream of almost boiling water until the pain suggests that cooling may be necessary.

- Select bar of soap and ensure that this is rotated quickly in the unaffected hand to avoid contamination of the soap itself.
- The soap will automatically become contaminated if the water splashes from the dirty hand to the clean hand. If this occurs, repeat until satisfactory brain signal is received.
- Should you manage to complete the task successfully, you may consider cooling.
- Should cooling be achieved, check hands for suitable redness and walk away quickly, or repeat procedure to apply greater pain and discomfort.

Important note: Be aware that this could develop into a lifelong activity and despite the obvious difficulties you may face, you must continue to hide this from the world. Your hands may suffer to the extent that they bleed but you can always use the excuse that you have a skin problem.

- Be prepared to experience time management issues and in particular you must recognise that being late is standard practice when following this procedure.
- Realise that the family won't notice, probably because they are too busy getting on with life.
- Recognise that the only opportunity for change will be when you are offered an alternative compulsion or more extreme intrusive thoughts.
- You could always select a new obsession, but be assured that it will no doubt select you in due course.
- Be comforted in the fact that washing hands is the least of your worries.

I remember the old saying 'cleanliness is next to godliness'. If only it were true.

The washing hands thing has long gone, well, I say long gone, that's not strictly true, but in terms of how much stress it causes and the consumption of time by ritualistic, repetitive motions, I guess you could say it is insignificant. The excrement dilemma remains to this day and applies a certain amount of pressure each time it enters my conscious mind.

Thinking back, there was the time shortly after I joined the Fire Service in 1986, that my pump (fire engine) was mobilised to a chimney fire in one of the areas of our patch where, let's say, residents were less socially aware than one would consider to be reasonable.

You come across all manner of wonderful, quirky and often downright strange people in my line of business. Over the years I have become eternally grateful for the extreme experiences and unexpected exposure to the abnormal that most people rarely get to witness. The lessons to be learned by merely engaging with and serving all levels of society in critical, often sad and in some cases comical circumstances cannot be underestimated and for me at least, the learning continues to this day.

The chimney was well alight as we approached, and to cut a long story short we got to work both inside and outside the property. Standard procedure: a dual-pronged attack to the hearth and the roof. Suffice to say the dog mess came back to haunt me when I was least expecting it and at a time when it could cause considerable embarrassment; for me, not the occupiers. Shall we say that the house was a little on the grimy side and indeed it was clearly customary for the pet dogs to evacuate their bowels inside the property rather than outside in the fresh air.

Since then I have become all too familiar with dogs making a meal of their waste matter, but is this a more acceptable solution to the problem? Our two seemed to indulge quite regularly and although it may leave less to pick up at the end of each day, it did little to comfort my mind.

Being the cautious and meticulous individual that I am, I didn't really want to spread the dog faeces to the outside of the property, surmising at the time by means of observation that it was highly likely that the garden was reserved for old settees, scrap cars and empty beer cans. I trod carefully between door and fireplace whilst all the time (being British) not wanting to embarrass myself by admitting I found the conditions horrifying and refusing to continue. I was a firefighter and battling adversity was nothing to me, and to be honest the rest of the crew found the situation hilarious, whilst at the same time slightly troubling. My boots were caked by this point, despite my best efforts and so, on receiving the order to get on the roof and squirt water down the chimney, I trotted outside imagining that I would have required gymnastic ability to avoid contamination and therefore I should grin and bear it.

Despite my professional pride and fear of being found out, I became increasingly stressed by the predicament and the concern that in just a few hours I would no doubt be sharing a quantity of this filth with my family. What you need to remember from the washing thing, is that this stuff can be fatal and virtually impossible to remove successfully, particularly if in your head you think you are deliberately trying to damage your nearest and dearest.

I was sweating heavily because of the thoughts going through my head and highly concerned that my demeanour would give the game away. I made my way up the ladder to the roof, rung by rung, depositing 'it' as I moved. The pantiles on the roof were able to take my weight and as it was a shallow pitch, accompanied by a jockey (probationer) I walked to the ridge with the hose reel, and both he and I held on to the chimney stack and applied water in the required manner.

Health and Safety hadn't been invented in the service at that time and the hassle of using a roof ladder and safety gear was some years away, so the major concern was always to get the job done. With the fire extinguished we turned away and were just about to descend the slope to the ladder pitched against the eaves when my partner remarked on the mess he had observed on the tiles.

'What's that lot?' he said.

'Don't know,' I said, innocently.

'It's dog shit,' said my mate.

'Is it?' I said.

'Jesus!' he said. 'How the bloody 'ell did a dog get up here?'

I believed he was serious and on asking him recently on his day of retirement from the service, he laughed at the recollection and reminded me that he was a bit 'thick' in those days. I still don't know if he had genuinely not realised what had caused it.

My smile and giggle disguised my intense distress as I considered how I would make it from the roof to the pump and how I would cope with the obligatory spray of water to the sole of my boots when what I really needed was a good half an hour with the hose reel at high pressure. There was definitely a need for full decontamination before leaving for home the next morning.

I would be delayed for at least an hour in the wash house scrubbing my Wellington boots and cork helmet. My wool tunic and yellow plastic leggings would also be bagged up and taken home to clean. The gloves would be thrown away and I would indent for a new pair, stating 'replacement due to fire ground damage'. The journey home would be dominated by the thought that I had deliberately not taken enough care, deliberately failed to decontaminate effectively and deliberately transported a hazardous substance to my home, to my two youngsters.

Walking through the door at the end of the shift the following morning, I flatly refused to cuddle my three-year-old daughter and six-month-old baby son until I had successfully eased the aching in my brain. Not until I had managed to convince myself that I was clean and no longer posed a threat to their health; no, to their lives. This type of incident would always serve as a reminder of how lucky I was in the early days when washing and checking was all that stood in the way of relative normality.

The standard was set, but perhaps without realising it I had found something to be considered for the future. Maybe, just maybe, I could use the power of distraction to prevent the worst of my disabling thoughts breaking me down. Perhaps by altering my mindset at the point where I recognised the onset of a downward spiral, I could focus on the less intrusive issues such as this. I knew I could handle such things by using simple replacement tactics. I was sure that the professionals would see this as a defeatist approach, but for me it was a form of therapy.

That said, the respite from the hours spent washing and cleaning was most welcome but as the vacant space is always quickly and suitably filled by more sinister and distressing challenges, it is almost too automatic to fight. I think it is fair to say that I was destined to spend my life between sanity and varying degrees of being extremely close to the edge. For many years now I have had a suspicion that the majority of us walk a very thin line between being categorised as sane or hastened into the world of madness.

The more I saw during my working life between human nature and my infrequent exposure to mental health professionals, the more I realised that the evidence makes that suspicion become more plausible. Could it be that spending so much time trying to mend the troubled mind, allows the negative thoughts of the patient to transfer to the carer? This must be so, as in my experience I have often felt that the most qualified and experienced of those commissioned to help me have left me thinking that the safer option would be for me to walk away and fend for myself.

The quirks that each of us possess have only to be influenced by a traumatic, painful or extreme event to move us to the other side. The individual traits that make us special in one area can destroy us in another and result in a meltdown. We are all one step away from disaster and the brightest flames can be extinguished with a small unexpected gust of wind.

5. Secondary school is the beginning of the rest of my life.

Tough times ahead, especially for high achievers I was told. The sport was going to be good after success in the first year. Oliver Weirdo actually won the trophy for the most successful athlete at the end of summer term sports day. Short-lived, unfortunately, because after collecting the 'Victor Ludorum' trophy for outstanding athletic achievement, it took a brief period of 'down' time to realise that I had only been successful because I'd entered more events than anyone else and scored points in each of them.

I did win the high jump, which was a pretty amazing feat looking back. Smallest boy in the year winning the high jump, has to be incredible, doesn't it? Not really, as none of the talented athletes entered; it must have been just the geeks and no hopers. Of course the other reason is that I was the oldest in the year as my birthday is September. I had been twelve for nearly a year by sports day and that surely steeped the odds in my favour considering some of the boys had barely reached that milestone. What a huge advantage that gave me. Without doubt, everyone thought I was more than a little lucky.

Billy Holder; I really didn't get on with him. He would always ignore me in school and I thought we had a lot in common. Both of us were keen footballers, only he was talented and I just tried hard to be talented.

The sports day had left a residual buzz around the school and people were practising in the long jump pit. I was doing my bit as a budding triple jumper and Holder was showing off, jumping the furthest and looking in my direction with a glimmer of sympathy on his face.

He had a bit of a reputation for being handy with his fists, according to my friends who had attended the same junior school. I, too, could handle myself as Dad had been so ashamed of me that he made me do judo lessons to toughen me up. Being small, blond and pretty, how would I ever achieve anything? Being a strapping truck driver made him an authority in that respect.

The judo did help as I soon became one of the top fighters in my age group in the county. It helped when I got picked on at school too and allowed me to get something of a reputation myself. This tended to make people avoid picking a fight with me. Not Holder though; he smirked and came right over and barged into me. I think it was a deliberate shove, but I just pushed back to show that in my eyes he had no credibility. He fell over and I walked away. Good job it was Friday, though I knew Monday morning would bring that shove back to haunt me. He was a big lad and maybe next week when back at school I would be feeling vulnerable.

Monday never came. Not for poor Billy Holder at least. Tragically he lost his life in a canoeing accident on a notorious stretch of the local river. He fell in whilst enjoying the summer sunshine when he and two mates capsized their Canadian canoe. Billy (I had better call him that now out of respect) was a strong swimmer whereas the two other lads were not. They survived.

Assembly on Monday morning was dark and frightening. That innocuous push on Friday afternoon had somehow played a big part in the loss of a young life. It would haunt me for years to come. This seemingly random event in my life is something I now believe was the kick start that my brain had been waiting for to send it into permanent overdrive. Because the poor lad had died and because I couldn't accept that it was absolutely nothing to do with me, it was the point at which death and harm became a virtually permanent fixture in my brain.

6. Reassurance is the key.

The events of that summer weekend should not have been etched in the brain of a young boy for anything other than the absolute sadness one would associate with the loss of a young, innocent life. I understood that, but the chemicals in my brain were unable to accept the rationale and the crossed wires meant that the signals defaulted to self-destruction. To you, it is a simple black and white question, but to me it was impossible to determine what was reality and what may have been testament to my personal peculiarities. I needed reassurance in some way and how I was going to achieve that was impossible for me to imagine.

It was very difficult to approach anyone with such feelings. That may sound strange because surely if I needed to speak to someone about it, then I obviously knew it was a stupid, childish phase that I needed to outgrow. It was not as simple as that: I sort of knew it was irrational, but on the other hand it was extremely real and it frightened me to the extent that without confiding in someone, I knew I would not be able to look forward to any kind of future.

Before long I was seeking reassurance from many sources: family, close friends, even strangers, depending on the circumstances. This was, I felt, the best way to deal with the insecurities, fears and indecision that grew exponentially. The cool thing is that I became so good at getting what I needed that everyone continued to miss the signs and, as I understand now, viewed the continuing barrage of questions and seemingly pointless observations as a sign of my intelligence and of an especially enquiring mind. This made me feel better too, as rather than look at myself as different, I could rejig it as an indication of my being special in some way.

The main problem was that at this stage in my young life I could never tell which came first in driving the cycle of never-ending peaks and troughs of mood. Was it the battering from constant 'horrible thoughts' as I called them, or was it the depressive state in which I regularly found myself? Did the thoughts make me depressed or was the depression the unseen force behind the thoughts? Sometimes, even now, I fail to recognise the timing and to be honest I think it's random and unpredictable, making understanding and dealing with it all the more difficult.

Popular television would have you believe that OCD is simply an illness confined to the home and always relating to domestic issues. This may largely be true, little do I know, but the washing and cleaning and hoarding aspect is only the tip of an enormous iceberg. The spectrum for OCD sufferers can be extremely broad and varied. Programmes like *Obsessive Hoarders* and *Obsessive Compulsive Cleaners* have, I believe, almost glamourized the illness but I can assure you that to those diagnosed with OCD and the clinical depression that often complements it, glamorous is not a word that trips from the tongue.

7. Green pound notes.

New Year's Eve was upon us, and I looked forward to it with anticipation after another unrewarding Christmas. Being short of money and possessions was not so much something that concerned me, more that this represented my first real opportunity to start to finance some of the things that I had seen other teenagers find so easy to gain. Well, that was the way I saw it anyway.

Few jobs for my age group were available unless you were fortunate enough to have the only paper round in the village or managed to know the right people to give you some farm work over the school holidays. There was nothing else for it then, I would have to do some babysitting for neighbours. I was fourteen years old and I always had a rapport with the mums and dads on the estate, being consistently polite and friendly on the outside whilst being extremely unhappy on the inside.

There were always plenty of offers in those days to look after small children for a number of local families but I had never really had the inclination, considering the activity to be a girl's job. Finally I relented and agreed to spend December 31st at someone else's house minding four children, the youngest being two years old and the eldest only eight. This, for me, was a daunting but exciting prospect because it meant that by merely watching television on my own for a few hours I would earn a few quid, eat biscuits and drink fizzy pop and not even have to deal with the small people as they would all be safely tucked up in their beds before Mum and Dad left for the party.

'Back just after midnight', they said as they left and all was quiet as I settled into the 1960's sofa and wondered what was on TV. This was going to be too easy, I thought, and decided what I would do with the money in the New Year. Probably save it and wait until I had enough to go to the market and buy some Dr. Marten boots (the sort that Alexei Sayle sang about in the '80s). It would be the first time I would ever have something that I didn't desperately need and, more to the point, something all the cool people had been seen wearing for ages.

The evening passed quickly and I looked forward to going home across the road, merely a stone's throw away. I thought it was about time that I went upstairs and checked that all the kids were OK as I had heard nothing for a couple of hours. The oldest two were in the one room and both were sleeping soundly. The little girl was in her own room and murmured as I opened the door. Waiting a few seconds whilst she settled, I moved towards her bed and placed her covers up to her shoulders. Just for a moment a feeling of dread hit me like a sledgehammer. Oh my God, what if I had moved the covers up too far and she suffocated while I was sitting downstairs none the wiser?

I felt sick immediately and wondered what I should do with the sheets. Should I move them down? But what if she got cold and somehow that made her ill? What if, what if, what if? The thoughts were coming thick and fast and I knew that whatever I decided to do, my actions would be irrelevant because in my mind there was obviously some wicked intent.

The feeling of paralysis, numbness in my arms and legs and inability to make sense of the messages reaching out to my limbs, increased the feeling of nausea. What if the little girl woke to see me looking at her and in the confusion of her sleepiness she felt the need to cry, to shout or to scream? I must have looked like an intruder and my unfamiliar face in the semi-darkness would look exactly like the monster my brain was trying to make me believe I was. The type of monster who hurts small children.

I went into the parents' room and tried to forget what I had imagined as I needed to make sure that the toddler snuggled in the enormous bed was safe and well. Walking into the room I quickly forgot the panic stricken feelings of a few seconds earlier as I could not hear her breathing. I had to lean closer to the bed to put my ear to the tiny nose and mouth. Was that a breath? No I didn't think so. Closer still, until my face touched the little cheeks. Yes, that was definitely a breath but my face got too close. I touched the little girl. That must have been deliberate and I was obviously a pervert. Panic, fear and disgust all at the same time. I could not cope.

The fleeting thoughts of the previous few minutes hit me as I went quickly down the stairs. It must be that I had done something terrible to one of the children. No, it actually meant that I was simply fighting to stop myself from killing a child. Yes that was it. I really was that person that I had worried about on so many occasions before. It was easier when I was in my own room and fighting while isolated, but this was so different. Thoughts of the busy road and the push in Mum's back, came rushing into my consciousness.

Torment as I waited for hours and hours. Why weren't they back yet? It was 1:00 a.m. and New Year had come and gone. Didn't they know that they had left their precious things alone with a monster? I curled up on the sofa and tried hard to shut everything out. This could not be what I was. I cried a little and wondered where I would be if this carried on. Would I ever have children and if I did would they be safe? The test card showing the sweet little girl, a blackboard, and a weird clown face on the tired old TV, bore into my brain long after programmes ended.

Drained and broken in body and spirit, I checked on the children one more time when the clock had sluggishly moved to 4:00 a.m. The task was made simpler by the fact that I blanked off my mind and wandered through each room, only aware of my own heavy heartbeat as I moved. They were all fine, I registered on autopilot.

I hadn't enough energy to fight anymore. I think the defeat I had suffered at the behest of my own conscience had resulted in the first of many severe bouts of self-hatred and deep depression. For a fourteen-year-old it was hard to take and looking at the two inebriated parents ten minutes later as I left for home, I knew that something had to be done. They were oblivious, but I decided that I would never babysit again as I pocketed the four pound notes. Not enough to buy one Dr. Martens boot, let alone a pair.

Back home and the house was silent, no one to talk to and a future that promised more of the same. That line of work was definitely not my vocation. That said, I got the feeling that life may not be for me either. The poem I penned truly defined my frame of mind and I believe this was the first time that I ever considered ending my life. I didn't know how I would do it, but the message was loud and clear. Later, raising the issue once more with my responsible adults I again failed to gain an insight into the workings of my mind.

8. Respite for the Human JCB.

Life, to my surprise, unexpectedly and thankfully began to change for me around this time as my penchant for all things sporty once again came to the forefront of daily activities. My ability as a budding footballer received a boost as I played regularly for school and local teams and was also selected to represent the area schools side. This meant that my focus became more and more centred around fitness and making sure that I would not make a fool of myself. I keenly sought to learn more about my version of 'replacement' or 'distraction' therapy. The regular and consistent expenditure of energy was soon to become an extremely satisfying and sometimes exhilarating means of balancing out my life. By diverting my attention from the demons, creating a focus for overactive brain activity and increasing my physical awareness and fitness, the football had provided an escape route, at least for the moment. Don't get me wrong, there was still time for ritualistic washing, checking and questioning, and to some extent the daily training was obsessive and compulsive, but I couldn't hurt anyone could I?

This new lease of life was also bringing fresh challenges in the shape of an offer from a local builder who thought it would be in my interests to do some manual labour for him. Clearly this would be 'on the cheap' as I was fourteen years of age and it was only during holidays and weekends, but the lure of money for new clothes was much too good an opportunity to miss.

The beautiful, seemingly never-ending summer of 1976 saw me sweltering in the heat whilst I channelled out trenches and dug holes for a middle-aged man who watched and I believe, admired, as a pocket dynamo completed the work that he was in no fit state to attempt. Rather portly I think may be the kindest description, and what fair-minded and self-respecting carpenter would labour for a living? He created my second nickname and one I much preferred to the 'Bronco' tag because it meant that I was good at something and everyone else would know too, once they heard it through the grapevine. I was a 'human JCB'. Not bad for fourteen eh?

The 1976 heat wave remains one of the hottest and driest summers since Met Office records began in 1914. It had been the warmest of the 20th century until some twenty years later. From May through until October I earned my new, trendy clothes and shoes and built up some resistance to the constant pressure of OCD and bouts of depression. Not aware of these labels at the time and not being in a position to investigate, I continued blindly, hoping that if I tried hard enough it would all go away.

Knowing what I know now I could have done some research because my school was one of the first in the country to install computer technology. At that time it needed a small classroom to accommodate the hardware, the intelligence of which can now be squeezed into any mobile telephone. I had recently started my CSE computer studies course, but this was more linked to standard languages of the day such as Binary, Algol, COBOL and FORTRAN and a little low level programming. Playing on the three white boxes available was strictly limited to curriculum activities and I was by no means an expert.

If only . . . maybe I would have recognised and dealt with the cause and effect, but in honesty I think any knowledge at that time would have been more of a burden than a blessing.

The summer had been a good period for me and my hopes were high for my final years of school, a time when plans needed to be made regarding my long-term future. My mind had been considerably more relaxed during the last few weeks of my employment, when my benefactor asked me to help him erect a shed at the top of his garden. We worked all day with me holding and fetching and carrying, much like the manner to which I had become accustomed at home. I was happily going about my business when he passed me a hammer. Holding the four-inch nail in one hand and the hammer in the other I proceeded to hit and miss as you would expect when attempting a new skill. He leaned in towards the wooden side panel to assess the area for damage and just for a second my mind wandered into a 'what if' scenario. I knew his head was too close to the swing of my arm and the hard metal lump attached to it.

What if I missed my target and accidentally hit his head? How would I explain that away? No one could possibly believe that it had been an accident, and anyway it would probably be a deliberate attempt by me to deceive the authorities, to get away with murder. It was a crazy way to think, but I found myself dwelling on the thoughts with such an intensity that I felt my heart pounding, racing, and all the time feeling a terrible dread throughout my entire body. The fact that I liked this man, a man who was unwittingly offering himself up for sacrifice at the hands of the innocent-looking child, made absolutely no difference to the way in which my brain mapped out the end of his life.

I was terrified, disgusted and heartbroken at the same time and the more I tried to remove the thoughts from my mind, the deeper I sank into desperation. I knew the thoughts were wrong and I knew they were not an indication of any genuine intentions, but their mere presence created a devastating vision and I had to face the realisation that I would always be trapped in this dangerous world. Things had somehow become far more serious in my mind, because now there was the additional threat of weapons. I was too inexperienced, too naïve, and understood too little about my condition to be able to defend myself. I was unable to anticipate and avoid the onslaught that I would surely face. With the advantage of hindsight, I now realise it was around this time that I began to walk blindly into areas of OCD that I could never have imagined.

9. Growing up fast or remaining a child.

Surely the pressure of teenage life, studying, and the obvious demands of the transition from childhood to manhood would create paths to alternative thought processes? Could it be that my experiences were just a phase, something that all teenagers faced, perhaps not as extreme in most cases but nevertheless normal and nothing to worry about? Surely my developing interest in girls and the fact that I had always been popular in that respect would enable me to focus fully on something pleasurable for a change and just maybe, the memories that my intrusive thoughts had created would be banished from my mind for good.

Thus, girlfriends became very important to me, as I imagine they are with most teenage boys. My previous fears had created huge barriers in my brain but I was able to use the painful experiences as a warning, a reminder to teach my mind, at least temporarily, to focus on something else. Schoolwork took second place and the pleasure of having a pretty girl in my life remarkably eased the pain I had become familiar with. Relationships were all innocent in the sense that I always preferred the nice girls and although opportunities to date the more promiscuous were tempting, I guess my nature predicted my preferences in that respect.

During my fourth year at secondary school I moved out of the family home and into my Gran's house, for no reason other than wanting a break from home. It seemed like a good idea at the time anyway. Gran, my Mum's mother, was very homely and welcomed me with open arms. Strange really, because as a very young boy I had always assumed that she was more focused on the girls (my sisters) than me and because I was the only boy, I was something of an enigma to her. She was used to girls I surmised, because she was mother to two daughters and had sadly lost two infant boys many years earlier. It was a common event in those days and because of these earlier tragedies I assumed she felt some bitterness towards me.

Whilst living at Dingle Mill I found the truth was quite the opposite. I discovered that despite her hard-looking face and coarse, rasping voice, which I suspected was a side effect of the heavy smoking that she and my grandfather enjoyed immensely, she was extremely fond of me and was more than a little flattered by my decision to jump ship and spend some time with them both.

Moving to the old mill house and stables was almost like going to a country retreat, away from the tedium at home where my mind had been so preoccupied with my problems that I had forgotten how to lead a normal life. The house was not their own but they had lived there for many years as tenants and although needing some tender loving care to restore it to its former glory, it was a pleasant and charming place to spend some time. I was able to function more comfortably because although the solitude brought an increase in the basic ritualistic behaviours such as reciting bedtime safety lists, overpoweringly obsessive personal hygiene standards and repetitive physical rituals, it also strangely released me from the vice-like grip of soul destroying, intrusive thoughts.

Gran and I were regularly alone and I think I can safely say that at no point did I venture into the 'what if' scenarios that had such a devastating impact on my life. To some extent I think I used the respite as an excuse to wallow in my own self-pity and, apart from snogging girls in the old stables and doing the odd bit of school homework, I self-debated my reason for being and decided that maybe a life of relative solitude would be the answer to all my troubles. I wrote lots of poetry and felt better about myself because the poetry, all pretty much depressing stuff, allowed me to express how I felt and I didn't have to tell anyone or share my mood. I suppose it would appear to some that I almost used the change of lifestyle to run away and wrap myself in a safety blanket of isolation and large helpings of 'feeling sorry for myself'. Gran didn't mind though, as we had some really meaningful conversations and I learned a lot about growing up.

Some years later, one awfully insensitive and abrupt psychiatrist destroyed that illusion as he plainly told me that my problem was largely based on the fact that I hadn't grown up and the OCD was nothing but childish thoughts. Good job I only met him once as he was a replacement for my previous shrink and clearly knew nothing of OCD and had forgotten how to use his bedside manner in a constructive way.

Sadly most of the poetry seems to have been mislaid apart from the few verses already shared with you. Probably a bonus though, as it wouldn't have cheered anyone's spirits or provided evidence that my outlook may have improved in time. To me, however, mentally I had improved already and I guess that begged the question that if I could do it once, then surely I could do it all the time. It has taken me many years to realise that in order for me to feel well there are many intangible elements.

Having a beautiful, kind and caring family, enough money to live comfortably, a great job and fulfilling hobbies and interests are often irrelevant when these intangible pieces of the jigsaw enter the puzzle and have the potential to make or break in an instant. The timing is crucial; the downward spiral of depression has to be halted before it suffocates your mind and wraps up your arms and legs, the feel-good chemicals in the brain and body have to be at the optimum level and the focus of your mind must steer you towards positivity.

Negative and self-destructive thinking can have a devastating effect. It's rather like reaching a point of no return without recognising danger checkpoints along the way, a position where positive mental attitude is powerless. When you face the endless barrage that OCD delivers it's so easy to forget how you coped the last time your state of mind hit the critical stage. If that happens, all the previously tried and tested coping strategies become useless and you have to simply ride out the storm.

I am not sure quite how long my sabbatical lasted but it was a period in my life when I was on a high for longer than usual, and this gave me hope. You must appreciate that seeking external help had not even entered my head, and with little guidance or support I would wait another ten years or more before that option would become a reality.

Could anyone have helped? Should anyone have advised? Why was I left to suffer in silence? These questions remained unanswered because in those days we just didn't know what we were dealing with. That aside, for two years I felt that I made great strides in banishing some of my worst memories to a far off place where they became vague and unimportant blips in my development. I don't know if I really believed it but the best I could hope for was that it was all part of growing up.

One more attempt at babysitting followed. This proved to be a step too far as the old thoughts and feelings returned with a vengeance. No one could understand why I turned down the offer of regular lucrative evenings sitting in a house owned by the managing director of a huge company, and lifts home in a Porsche Carrera, merely for minding a privileged child with impeccable behaviour and manners. Naturally, as a sixteen-year-old, I was unable to explain the real reason for my reticence and I suspect my parents assumed I was the stereotypical waster.

My early years had been influenced by varying degrees of poverty and perhaps I was reacting to feelings of envy, unable to accept the lifestyle of a child only a few years my junior. Would this be a reason for having incredible urges to harm that child? The feelings were generated by mere thoughts with no notion of how to act on them, no method, not even a fleeting idea of how I could or would cause harm. The fear created by just the image was enough to bring me down to earth and wonder how I would ever function in the real world. Sixteen years old and totally debilitated by something that wasn't even tangible.

Real desire to end my life became a regular and prominent visitor to my mind. Looking back now, I don't know how I managed to hold things together, because I had absolutely no one that would understand. I knew I couldn't, nor ever would, act on my irrational thoughts but the nausea, pain and distress I felt, I can hardly describe. So why didn't I kill myself? If I was so frightened surely the best thing to do would be to rid the planet of any evidence of my existence. The answer to this question was always a mystery and remained so for many long years and it's only now that I may have discovered an answer. But the answer would not have been relevant then, as I truly felt I had no reason to live.

10. Flyboys.

The best thing I could do was join the armed forces. That sounded like a reasonable response to a difficult situation and the Royal Air Force careers office welcomed me with open arms. I was a bright, intelligent youth and my options were numerous. Having passed all tests I went for the mandatory medical, with no trepidation. The forms were completed, the tests were done, and the final discussion stood between me and a career that mirrored to some extent Dad's National Service. Before you ask, I wanted to join for me and not for him, and a yearning to leave my home life behind as soon as possible was the main influence.

Confirmation arrived through the letter box a few weeks later that I would not be permitted to join the RAF, as I had admitted to being a persistent bed wetter as a child. I had wrongly stated that this affliction had continued until I was eleven years old. In fact it had ceased by the time I was ten and was something that I had for many years pushed into the back of my mind; painful memories of something I could do absolutely nothing about and an honest admission of another little crack in my armour. I believe that this affliction was also something about which there was little medical knowledge.

My other granny once said that if I lived with her she would have cut off the appendage. That would stop me. She was my paternal grandmother and had been hardened and desensitised by years of living with six wayward boys and a daughter who through an error of judgement had become pregnant at the age of fourteen; illegitimate children were extremely shameful even in the lower echelons of society, I learned. I discovered many years later that in fact she had been very fond of me but was not quite so enamoured of Mum and my sisters, so I realised that the amputation idea had just been a joke for grown-ups.

So, having quickly cleared up the confusion (apparently age ten was the allowed cut off point, no comedy value intended, but those wetting the bed at eleven were not so fortunate), having packed and prepared, I set off on the train to Lincolnshire for a very short-lived career in the Royal Air Force. Six weeks at the training camp and true to form this young trainee managed to be sufficiently obsessive and committed to earn the great accolade of top recruit in Number Ten Flight. This was something of which I was momentarily proud but, as with all things special, I was obviously just lucky at the time and there were far more deserving cases. By the time the visiting Air Chief Marshall presented me with my certificate at the passing out parade my brain had already seized upon further opportunities to create havoc in my life.

Training at RAF Hereford, worries about success, friendships, relationships, previously encountered rituals and obsessions all now combined, ganging up in a huge, boiling pot of self-doubt and self-hatred. Was this what I wanted, could I really sign on for three, five, nine years given my psychological profile? For goodness sake, I had needed a last minute stay of execution merely to join the illustrious boys in blue and if it hadn't been for that awful buzzer thing I would have probably still been floating down my bed every night. Strange thing is that I have almost gone full circle now as I need the toilet as much at fifty three years old as I did then. The main difference being that I always manage to wake nowadays before relieving my bladder.

The buzzer contraption consisted of a rubber sheet through which was passed a small electric current, rather like an electric blanket. For six years, from age four to ten, it was a nightly event to be woken numerous times by a horrendous sound emitting from a control box that indicated moisture had been detected. The contraption didn't work particularly well given that by the time it activated, my spirits were normally well and truly dampened. Having said that, I guess it did sort me out eventually because the electrical impulse transmitted to the buzzer, sent an impulse from my inadequate brain to my bladder and back to my brain to wake me up in time to pee like normal humans.

This is something that I only recall now and have rarely considered over the years but is it possible that this six-year trial was just another outcome caused by crossed wires in the brain, chemical imbalance, psychological defect or genetics? Was it merely one of life's challenges? Something that we all face, but in different guises.

I now think it is not really so important what we face but how we react, learn and grow from our experiences. If anyone had said that to me at the time I would have no doubt smiled sweetly and walked away whilst being happy in the knowledge that there was at least someone crazier than me.

The older I get the more I recognise that perhaps the fine line between normal and otherwise becomes less defined. The difference between sane and insane, wacky and weird, strong and weak becomes less obvious. Many of us inadvertently follow a path, driven by fate, desire, greed, love, even in search of fame and stardom that will lead us to the edge and occasionally, just occasionally, tempt us to test the water in the deep, dark ocean of 'otherwise'.

Moving on and time was of the essence as a posting to RAF Valley in the cold, dark winter months was hardly the life I had expected. My dreams of Cyprus, Malta or some other sunny destination had been well and truly destroyed and a lack of accommodation on the main camp led to a temporary billet at an old, largely disused army camp at Ty Croes.

This was a remote outpost: rugged, bleak and forbidding. The location and environment was, for me, a stark reminder of all things negative in my world. Deep depression from the outset, much solitude and gloom, emotionally drained and, despite the efforts of two similarly aged recruits, I was unable to picture my future, unable to envisage how this environment could ever be conducive to my aspirations for a better life. Rituals and obsessive behaviour, constant intrusive thoughts and nights spent analysing my life led to trips to the edge of the world for me.

I stood motionless, looking out into the Irish Sea, waves crashing against the rocks under my feet, threatening to engulf me with every rhythmic surge and drag me to the depths. Nobody understood the way I felt and more importantly, nobody really cared. The dagger of reality was embedded deep in my heart but the road to salvation was here and now. My previous life had worn me down; family and friends, a simple phone call away, were unable to stop me. One small step would solve everything.

But I didn't do it, I walked away from the edge, deciding instead to take hold of my future once again, to be in control of my destiny, whatever that may be. To some I was no doubt weak to consider ending my life when so many people suffer real heartbreak and tragedy in their lives. I had temporarily accepted that I was worth more and though it may have seemed like another failure, I actually saw it as a small victory.

I handed in my resignation after five months of turmoil, because after six months in service it would have cost a considerable sum of money to buy myself out. My RAF career was over before it had really begun.

11. Here I am in bedsit land

Life continued and I found myself back at college, aiming for a business studies diploma. I had to do something to furnish myself with some hope that the future I had promised myself on Anglesey earlier in the year was not just my vivid imagination teasing me once again. The qualification would provide me with ample opportunities to choose my direction in life and I had decided that teaching, management or even a career in the legal profession would be within my grasp.

I can picture myself at the time, looking over the railings at the river's edge. It was dark and cold, and the oak trees lining the road outside my little bedsit cast eerie shadows all around me. The street lights broke through in patches and reflected off the water's surface. I was in a place that during my first eighteen years of life was extremely familiar and I knew the feeling would take a good while to move on and even then I would be left with the residual darkness that I feared would always be my shadow.

Living on my own and able to manage my own destiny was a huge advantage because as a mature student I qualified for a full grant from the education authority. The funding was enough to cover the eight pounds weekly rental of my single room with a sink, bed, Baby Belling twin hob and plenty of baked beans and corned beef.

There were shared bathroom facilities (not the best way to satisfy my hygiene concerns) and it was handy for college and work. My part-time job as a lifeguard at the local pool meant that I could make ends meet and I didn't need to spend every evening staring at the four walls or listening to The Cure on my record player. Funny, isn't it, how depressed people listen to depressing bands? Perhaps I was an eighties emo.

I had my first 'serious' girlfriend and my own place. Sounds great and in some ways it was, but as with all things great I somehow managed to create a short cut to 'not so great' in the blink of an eye.

I really don't know where the tipping point was between feeling sad and low, and feeling sad and desperate. College work, the pool and my girl all kept me fairly busy but when the dark clouds gathered there was no escape. I obsessed about college, wondering if I would ever manage to keep up the 70 per cent attendance target, and constantly struggling with the academic nature of the course. I couldn't really complain about going three and a half days a week but the extra hours at the pool meant there was too little time available for keeping up with the coursework. It was a fine balancing act between surviving and studying. Failure of the course was automatic if the attendance target was not reached but I had bigger things to worry about.

The smoking helped, because although it had taken all these years to realise the value of something I had detested as a child when breathing in Dad's second-hand fumes, I suddenly discovered its soothing and calming properties. Normal people would rightly consider this opinion to be somewhat delusional but it worked for me. Not in the way you may assume, as I hated the taste, the revolting sensation as it tracked from lips to lungs and the odious smell on my hands and clothes. I loved the exhale and the little rings I could blow after a little practice, but most of all I enjoyed the respite it gave my mind at difficult times. Being able to worry about accidentally setting fire to the house, the garden, almost anything was the perfect release from the thoughts of harming others. Failing that, my worries of what my girlfriend may be doing whilst I was not with her, just about provided sufficient distraction.

The family who owned the bedsits at the big house had three children and it was around this time that the youngest child seemed to become intrigued by me. She was only ten or eleven but very sweet and kind, unlike the rest of the family, but as soon as I noted her friendliness the poison started to rise, meaning I had to avoid her as much as possible. Hearing a light knock on the door early on Friday evenings and almost freezing with fear as I knew it would be the girl collecting the rent, I would open the door to about halfway and pass the money quickly, smile and thank her, then shut the door in case my thoughts took over.

Looking down at the river, my mind vibrated with a barrage of worries competing for a hearing. I worried that I may have dropped cigarette ash in my room and that the house would soon go up in smoke. I fretted over my girlfriend who, due to house rules, was not allowed to spend the night with me, and wondered if she was up to something at that time because I was unworthy and she was far too pretty for me. It would be natural for her to seek pastures new. I was probably rubbish in the sack anyway so who could blame her?

Concentrating on the fast flowing water I asked myself why I had such awful thoughts about the sweet girl, why I couldn't even face her properly and make her feel as welcome as she had made me feel. I wrestled with the question of whether my harmful thoughts were OK or if I deserved to be locked away. I knew at that time that it wouldn't be long before I would have to take the plunge for the safety of everyone.

Don't get me wrong; I knew deep down that these thoughts were just that and I had no conscious intention of acting on any impulse or urge. Sufferers don't do that, they just destroy themselves bit by bit, brain cell by brain cell. The chemicals in my brain were stronger than reasoning and sense. One day they would present me as a pragmatic, practically minded, intelligent, likeable and believe it or not, 'desirable' young man; the Oliver I occasionally saw in the mirror. The Oliver the chemicals would produce the following day was a scared and self-loathing individual who needed to end his life, not because he was a danger to anyone, except himself, but because he was unable to recognise that fact. The most vulnerable moments always came at the worst time. Which comes first: the worst time or the vulnerable moments?

The red box at the end of the line of trees was my only option on so many occasions during those late teen years at a time when I should have been growing and daring and broadening my horizons day by day. Sitting in my room on the worst days and nights, I wondered how I would manage to get over the gloom and despondency I was feeling. It seemed that every period of high was immediately and cruelly followed by an extreme low. I knew there must be something I could do to break this cycle and I hated myself for not realising that the whole thing was childish and immature and that I should just snap out of it like everyone else. The only thing for it was to enter the red box and phone home. My desperation meant that my doubts about the benefits of this leap of faith based on my struggles as a child, failed to deter me. I don't know what I ever said to Mum during those calls and I have no doubt that she worried and maybe even cried a little but the answers to my questions never came.

'I don't know what to do, I am so depressed that I cannot sleep, watch TV, read or relax. I can't even find the enthusiasm to seek refuge in the local pub.'

That's a thought. The drink idea never worked for me on the few occasions I attempted to drown my sorrows, to wallow in a drunken stupor, waiting to see if the clouds would lift. I learned quickly that alcohol was not the answer, not that I could ever take my beer, but I am relieved that the one vice familiar to many of my peers was not one with which I was able to engage. For me alcohol and depression did not combine to make a happy couple. Drink and OCD does not create an environment where life suddenly becomes joyous, and happy times do not lie teasingly at the bottom of a glass. I wondered if I should persevere a little longer with the demon drink, on the basis that it might just work next time. Years later I found that my theory was correct. My daughter had to learn the hard way when she tried to combine the two.

During those phone calls Mum tried to listen and advise but how do you prepare someone to battle an enemy that is unseen, is clever and unpredictable, sly, cunning and resourceful? She must have suffered considerably because she had to have known that there was no real answer to this strange preoccupation of mine. It was probably a relief that I had asked the same questions dozens of times in the past and nothing serious had happened to me so far. To her, my emotional calls could have been a result of my trying to adjust to life on my own.

'Come home and stay for a while,' she would say, knowing that with my commitments in the town, my life would need to be put on hold which would likely be a backward step. Boredom and inactivity would be the absolute worst outcome and going home would have been an admission of failure, and that would only serve to remind me that I would never be strong enough to be free. I looked out through the small panes of glass, smeared with grime from years of neglect, smelled the strong odour of what I sensed was stale urine soaking the concrete floor and opened the door to breathe in some fresh, cold air.

My eyes, red and bleary from tears and attempts to stop them, once again spotted the street lights reflecting off the water. It looked strangely inviting and soothing from here and I remembered there had been a time when I had almost succumbed to the power of nature and this made me wish that someone would come along and pick me up to launch me into the semi- darkness over the rails. That would be so much easier than contemplating my own way out. I reassured Mum that I would be fine and that I would call again when I felt better and promised that I wouldn't do anything silly. Putting the handset down I reminded myself that there were many ways to escape this life and now none of them seemed so terminal because I had been there many times before and now, here I was . . . just thinking about it. I thought I had been so close many times and asked myself what it was that had kept me alive when it seemed like happiness was beyond me?

I couldn't work out if my wishing to end it all was merely a cry to myself for help, or a genuine death wish. I decided it must be a way of banishing my awful thoughts to the furthest reaches of my brain and allowing room to imagine myself as a nice person. If I wanted to kill myself then it was obvious that I didn't want to harm anyone else, and as soon as I could return to dealing with the more mundane rituals and unnecessary evils that had become so familiar, the need for being concerned in other ways would temporarily fade away.

I had unwittingly discovered another string to my bow, another solution for the times when all seemed lost. Go to the edge of despair, compare the final solution to the threat of failing to act and move one step back from the edge and consider the risk of giving it one more chance. The benefits of a new high and the nice chemicals that brought would fortify and invigorate me ready for the next challenge. There would be worse times, but I must live and learn and hope for a miracle. I wondered if I could swap this for a physical illness?

I am reminded of the nights during my teenage years that I prayed to a God in whom I didn't believe. I had begged an unseen ally to provide a cure for my 'illness', whilst also bargaining with the non-existent benefactor for an alternative. I felt that a fair swap would have been the removal of my legs. This was by no means an inference that those with missing limbs were more fortunate than I, merely that for me it would be a fair and welcome exchange. Looking back and knowing what I know now, and even after having survived many difficult times, I would still opt for the amputations.

Some twenty years later I met a pretty thirty-something who recognised me from the house by the old telephone box. She was now married to a colleague and she fondly recalled the time when as a little girl she collected the rent from the young college man in the first-floor room. She reminisced that I was not like most people because I smiled, was polite and always paid on time. She spoke of how it was really funny when her mum and dad threw me out for breaking the rules on sleepovers, and she stated that my girlfriend had been a lucky girl.

I was proud of myself for seeming normal to others in bedsit land, and by her account I sensed that many such small successes had passed me by. I had missed so many opportunities to feel normal and good about myself and all that had been required was for me to interrupt my thought processes and look around. Sounds simple, and on good days it is, but as the old cliché goes, 'You are only as good as your last fight' and if you lose one, you have to get off the canvas and do your damnedest to win the next. Victories are so often short-lived.

12. Sexual encounters, children, marriage and some understanding.

My experiences have taught me that I need to ensure my mind is fully occupied, to stay as busy as possible. This seemingly straightforward task is proving to be exactly that, fairly simple, which is something of a pleasant surprise. Following the college years and a number of uncomfortably short-lived jobs trying to find my niche in life, I found myself stuttering from dead end to dead end with no apparent need for my O-levels and a hard-earned diploma in business studies.

Stumbling into anything that brought in some cash all I cared about was making ends meet and having the money to socialise and live from day to day. Lack of ambition allowed me to complete three seasons as a beach bum in Cornwall, working my passage as a grill chef in a Wimpy bar and spending my winters in the building trade and occasionally as a statistic on the unemployment register. The burger work in Cornwall and the free time during the day allowed me to acquaint myself with some of the more appealing aspects of growing up. Despite remaining a slave to rituals and obsessive behaviour the increased company of females helped me to avoid further desperate times for a while. This period of respite allowed me to build a little resilience before the exact same thing caught me cold and hit me with a disturbing retribution. My desire to please the fairer sex and to remain a valuable commodity in that department taught me to become an obsessive compulsive partner. This poisonous trait has proved to be another barrier to achieving a happy existence on so many occasions.

The winter work as a civil engineering ground worker – OK, a labourer – shovelling concrete and digging holes all day long, day in, day out, produced much in the way of happy brain chemicals. Recognising the buzz that this strenuous activity delivered I would challenge myself to shift as much concrete, lay as many pipes, slabs and kerbs as possible and load as many bricks and cement as my compact, muscular frame would permit within the working day.

Tools that could, in the wrong hands, create carnage were never considered to be weapons. My skills as a JCB and dumper driver, although fairly rudimentary, were never something that my brain associated with damage or harm. The façade of normality that was necessary to claim any sort of credibility in that male-dominated environment saw me pretending I was normal and at that time I guess I felt exactly that. I was part of the gang: alpha male, fit and physically healthy, and displaying a confidence with women that shaped my destiny more quickly than I imagined.

Fast forward to a hard day's graft, returning home to a newly pregnant partner and the thrill of knowing I would soon become a father. My own child, someone to cherish and nurture, to teach and to love, like I felt I had never been loved. That tough, cool image disappeared immediately I walked through the door of the little two-up, two-down terraced house, and the considerably louder and more confident personality faded away to reveal the old Oliver. At this stage the usual fears of harm from dirt, lack of cleanliness and normal household risks were amply supported by enormous feelings of insecurity. This manifested itself in a manner that has destroyed so many relationships and can present itself in many forms, all of them hugely damaging.

My insecurity led to an intensely possessive nature and I was unable to trust any partner for many years. I have to admit that at the time it seemed far more palatable for me to worry about the fidelity of my soon-to-be-wife than to return to the old me with thoughts that sought to destroy me. I settled for interrogation and accusations and was rarely satisfied with the response.

Don't get me wrong, there was absolutely no violence. Well, not from me at least, but in some ways I can't blame her for lashing out a few times at some of the things that I suggested may have occurred whilst my back was turned, out at work earning our crust and striving to support our newly formed family.

The worries grew and grew and eventually I found myself developing the negative side of the smoking compulsion to complement all the other abnormalities in my life. It failed to stop me smoking though, as I was convinced that it was something that could help me to maintain my sanity, allowing me to chill a little, calming me and allowing me the pleasure I deserved. No harm would come to my daughter as I was fanatical about her safety and her wellbeing, but my concerns about ash and smoke and related hazards far exceeded the benefits in which I had naively believed.

I was no longer employed and therefore not receiving the buzz from the strenuous activity, and it was blatantly obvious that the regular football matches at the weekend were unable to supply the quantity or quality of feel-good factor vibes that would fend off the inevitable. The football should have provided respite from the daily drudgery and the energy sapping nature of my condition. Many games passed in a blur as I spent most of the playing time repeating rituals and clarifying past events in my head. I can still see myself standing virtually motionless for long periods as I tried to make sense of the latest intrusive thought or the most recent attempt at proving myself to be the great protector rather than the ultimate betrayer. How I kept my place in the team is anyone's guess, but maybe the odd flash of skill or burst of terrier-like tenacity fooled anyone interested enough to care.

The inevitable happened and for at least two years I struggled with family life trying to be a good father and within a year an equally good husband, following a low-budget wedding. Gradually I took an ever increasing share of parental responsibility for my little girl. Nappy changing, feeding, playtime and bedtime were all things in which I needed to play a leading role in order to prove that I was worthy of such a position of responsibility. This followed the usual pattern of ritualistic behaviour, driven by obsessional and compulsive urges and the more I reassured myself of my good intentions, the need for further reassurance stacked the odds against me.

Was I feeding her properly and had I washed the feeding equipment effectively? Was there a risk that my actions could cause some harm, and was I taking all precautions to avoid being responsible for anything that could affect her survival? It sounds terribly dramatic but when you are unable to focus on very little else it's all terribly real.

My daughter had an Alice band that became very important to her and because I had still retained the smoking paranoia, one evening I sensed that some cigarette ash had accidentally made contact with it, and this had clearly been a deliberate act on my part. Rational thought was banished from my brain and the knowledge of the triangle of combustion was yet to be imparted and no doubt would have made little difference to my actions anyway.

I knew my priorities and also my absolute and undeniable love for her and therefore I needed to remove the risk of this cheap plastic item causing harm. Before going to bed that evening after mulling over my options for thirty minutes or more, I launched the Alice band as far as I could from the doorstep into a neighbouring garden. For a few minutes I felt relieved and confident that I had averted a disaster. Genuinely, this act had eased my mind considerably until I wondered if it may have created some other hazard for the poor family who had received the unexpected gift. Seemingly though, my extreme precautions had caused no harm to the neighbours. I was in the clear.

My daughter was the centre of my universe and it wasn't long before my wife forgot to take her contraceptive pill, falling pregnant once again. This forgetfulness seemed to occur roughly in a three-year cycle during our relationship.

In the meantime I found a certain amount of pleasure and respite from the standard family protection activities by allowing myself the freedom of the female world. Not something I am proud of but it seemed like a good idea at the time and certainly allowed me to understand the concepts of deceit and guilt in equal proportions.

Whilst participating in this extra-curricular activity my brain was elsewhere, trying to convince me that I was some kind of Lothario. In fact an equally, if not more accurate description, would be that of a weak liar. The moment I released the energy built up by the chase I felt the guilt and disgust of deceit. These were not feelings that I considered detrimental to my relationship as that had been in many ways dead and buried from the onset, my wife indulging in similar misdemeanours. No, the guilt was ever increasing by way of fear that it was harming my daughter and unborn son. This would be a recurring theme and the harm that I caused to my unborn son would hit me repeatedly, far into the future. So what should I have done: channel my desires in some other way or continue as a cheat to find what I must be looking for and suffer the consequences? It just seemed like I was on a hamster wheel of discovery. I knew every inch of that wheel but was unable to jump off and opt for reality.

Now an independent, bright and beautiful woman, I fear that my eldest daughter suffered at the hands of this doting yet inconsiderate father. Just today she explained from her temporary home in the Southern hemisphere that she feels as 'mad as ever' and although she manages to hide her real self from the world she speaks in terms that I recognise so well.

From a very early age she demonstrated signs of some form of mental illness but that rarely showed itself as OCD related. Nine years old and periods of counselling because of her sometimes inappropriate behaviour, failed to identify any specific patterns or causes of her obvious insecurity and sadness.

She grew up far too quickly and in some ways established herself as a woman of the world at a very early age, as had her mother. But what was the cause of this desire to venture into the adult world when barely a teenager; why would this pathway be her destiny? Did she choose to be this way or was it learned behaviour?

I know that the ever increasing ritualistic tendencies and bouts of depression failed her on many occasions and relationships were always short-lived and difficult. Rather than forcing upon her the intrusive thoughts to which I have become accustomed, she would (and still does) rule her life with counting and questioning. She seeks reassurance from everyone she meets, and thrives on incredibly intense highs whilst being debilitated by equally intense and frighteningly destructive lows. Her liking for alcohol often exacerbates these extremes.

Nature or nurture? Not being particularly sure about the value of research, aware that we are what we are, all I can really surmise is that it is probably a bit of both. Does OCD follow a specific pattern in families or perhaps depression comes first and then as a result of that initial injection of blackness, the learned behaviours take over as replacement for happiness and contentment?

American research has identified that a particular gene appears to be significant in families where clinical depression affects multiple members. They all have this specific gene and whilst it is recognised that a combination of genes may be responsible it is expected that a person with a parent or sibling who suffers from this disorder is five times more likely to develop similar symptoms. By the same token some British research indicates that this may be up to three times as likely. My understanding is that children also have a habit of picking up on certain depressive tendencies of the parent and this can result in the learned behaviour that presents itself in later life.

Research determines that OCD and depression are linked and the feel-good chemical, serotonin, appears to have a major influence in that respect. The long held opinion that a serotonin imbalance (and other associated chemicals and genetic traits) may be responsible for playing a part in the forming of these brain disorders has influenced treatment strategies for many years[1]. It remains a relatively unproven concept and it is debatable as to whether depression reduces serotonin levels or low serotonin levels influence the onset of depression.

There is absolutely no doubt in my mind that I am at least in part responsible for my daughter's difficult life. She didn't ask to be my daughter, nor did she expect to see her life through permanent filters that obscure reality. But whom do I blame, because I too was thrust head first into this world of insecurity and, some would say, immaturity? I remind myself that no one had depression or OCD before me. Why do I know that? Because the illness did not exist in those days. Mum always said that I burst out of her womb in a hurry, that I didn't want to wait for a more cultured and serene birth. Perhaps she forgot to mention that I jettisoned on to the hard quarry-tiled floor, head first, damaging that all important rational part of my brain. That must be the answer.

[1] Healthline.com, written by Stephanie Faris

13. Dream job.

The chances of my achieving anything other than mediocrity in the workplace had long been established as fairly low. I was said to be too much of a risk, had never managed to hold a job for longer than a few months, and was unlikely to succeed due to appearing to have butterfly syndrome.

This statement had been made by a senior officer following an unsuccessful interview for the Fire Service a couple of years earlier. The evidence is there in black and white, written in my personal record file. Merely passing all physical, academic and psychometric tests was a genuine achievement in those days. I was one of over a thousand applicants for six jobs in what had become a treasured occupation following the infamous industrial action of 1979 when the Army deployed Green Goddesses to keep our communities safe. The huge increase in pay as a result of that action along with my perception that to be a 'hero' would be a fine way to prove my worth to society and my family had me believing that my place above mediocrity was well and truly in the bag.

My attempts to land employment with a decent income and at least the potential for a little kudos had been scuppered by someone who was unable to use the correct phrase to describe me. His interpretation of someone with 'butterfly syndrome' was exactly opposite to reality. It actually relates to an urban dictionary meaning of someone with an extremely short attention span or who flits from one subject to another. On the contrary I was extremely focused, maybe on the wrong things, but nevertheless focus was not my issue. I assumed he was referring to my failure to remain in any previous post for longer than a few months and that my obvious propensity for itchy feet was similar to the movements of a butterfly flying from flower to flower, drinking the nectar and moving on to the next.

Perhaps I was a butterfly in those days but only on the surface. My insistence on maintaining the rituals and protective compulsions that kept my children safe was intense. It had to be, because in my head if I ever failed in my quest, I might as well have deliberately harmed them myself. In fact the tremendous pressure to maintain that kind of commitment particularly when new compulsions came along so often, always got me in the end. The familiar decline that saw me question my love for the two most precious things in my life was the hardest thing to bear and the one thing that I knew could destroy me completely. Logic and common sense were worthless and when the desperation began to build, there was no stopping it.

By unexpected good fortune I found myself at another final interview for the Fire Service and the chance to show my mettle, to achieve my true vocation. I thought back to my life as a sixteen-year-old in the village, sitting around a small, round table in the lounge of a cosy, low-ceilinged Tudor cottage with an assortment of ordinary village children.

14. Séance – a signpost to the future.

There were six of us, all of tender years and searching for some guidance in life. How we expected something as rudimentary as this amateur séance to be the font of all knowledge, heaven knows, but it seemed like a good idea at the time.

The usual silly questions were asked, like who was going to marry whom and who was going to turn out gay, and so on. The marriage thing was flavour of the month as my best mate at the age of seventeen had managed to sleep with a 'lady' who was married with two children. Suddenly she found herself in the divorce courts, but he seemed determined to settle down with his new, ready-made family and act like a real man. In our eyes he was a superhero, but not so to his mum and the rest of the village, and certainly not to the husband and two small children. The poor lad had slept in his clapped-out old car for several months while the dust settled, but by this time he was living in sin with his 1970's cougar.

I didn't have a clue how these things worked and just joined in to make up the numbers.

Mother Goose led the proceedings and we finally got on to what we would all be doing in the future. The glass moved slowly from letter to letter on the little table, spelling out an assortment of ridiculously unbelievable scenarios such as he is going to end up in jail, she will be pregnant by next year and the village idiot will become a brain surgeon as long as he studies hard. Not an exact version of events but you get the idea.

Problems arose, though, when the obsessive Oliver started to believe some of the weird and wonderful outcomes as I became very concerned when the Ouija board predicted that someone's sister would drown in a flood. Lo and behold, who was the only one at the table with a sister? Yes that's right, it was me and I actually had four of them and it could be any one of four. Apparently it was the one that now lives in America so I am still wondering after almost forty years if I still need to worry. Believe me, for a number of years it frequently popped up in my mind and raised genuine concerns.

The most intriguing prediction was that I would become a firefighter. Me, all five feet two inches of me. This was pre-RAF days and I hadn't started growing yet.

I knew at the time that you had to be big and strong and at least five feet six inches in height so this had to be a joke. I remember thinking how ridiculous these séance things were and despite having some nagging doubts about my sister's survival, particularly as the River Severn was only a stone's throw from the little cottage, I virtually forgot about my future vocation. That was until my initial attempt to join the service was thwarted at the final hurdle and I realised that knowing my luck, the chances of being in a position to try again would be slim.

But the slim chance had arrived and after making sure I was fitter than I had ever been I broke the record for the fastest mile they could remember during the initial fitness tests. Little old me was the fastest out of all the applicants, but then again I had trained like a Trojan and had the unfair advantage of being older than most at nearly twenty five, and had recently been earning a few quid playing football. No wonder I was a speed machine; I had even cheated in the fitness stakes.

The academic and psychometric tests were easy once again and I literally breezed the interview with a particularly pleasant senior officer. The height challenge was going to be difficult as I narrowly fell beneath the minimum height requirement, but this was my destiny, wasn't it?

One pair of extremely thick white sports socks later and a little stretch of the Achilles tendons made up the extra quarter of an inch and I was in. I was going to be a firefighter, nothing could go wrong and, aside from a little guilt about cheating the height test, I was more than happy. This would be the start of a new life, a wonderful opportunity to be someone, to earn a decent wage, plenty of excitement and self-respect, and a fresh start.

The man who had the measuring remit told me some years later that he knew I was slightly too short but he liked my spirit and tenacity. But I still knew I was a cheat!

15 Cure.

My relationship with doctors and psychiatrists had always been fairly unpredictable. Some good, some not so good. Terribly difficult over the years to find a general practitioner that behaved as if they genuinely understood and had a good grasp of the signs and symptoms of depression, let alone the intricacies of OCD. Recent experience has been significantly better than most over the years. The new lady doctor was willing to listen and not prejudge, and she seemed to have an awareness of the specific areas of the disorder that I presented without making assumptions, providing a vague diagnosis or suggesting unrealistic solutions. The usual ones being, 'I think we will try to increase your medication,' or, 'Let's try you on something else, you have been on Clomipramine for such a long time'.

Being honest and admitting too much to members of the medical profession had on previous occasions been a frightening proposition. How could I tell all to a new doctor, a stranger, when they would surely want to lock me away for the good of my family and the wider population?

Despite my gut feeling that this lady with the decent bedside manner was different to so many in the past, I had yet to find the courage to tell her face to face of my greatest fears, deciding instead (with her blessing) to pass on many of the more painful memories by sharing some of my early notes for *Ordinary Childhood Dreams*.

The doctor made an unexpected telephone call to my wife whilst I was at work saying that she had read the script and wanted to speak to me as soon as possible. My immediate and fleeting thought was that maybe she knew how to cure me or at least could provide me with some much needed positive guidance. In that brief moment my heart pounded with anticipation only for my brain to advise me of the futility of my hopes a few seconds later. Disappointment was not an unfamiliar concept for me, but when she simply congratulated me on my ability to function so well in both my career and as a family man despite my illness, my heart sank and my eyes filled without warning.

A while later, looking in the mirror I saw a man so many years older than my age and I came to the conclusion that I was just no good at life. Tears fell for the rest of that day because sometimes it just happens that way. I reminded myself that grasping for the improbable will regularly result in failure. Reaching for the impossible speaks for itself.

16. Exciting times ahead?

The excitement and trepidation I felt as I embarked on that journey up the M6 to the Fire Service training school in Chorley, Lancashire in May 1986 was something I hadn't expected to feel. I was in a position of strength as I had already completed military basic training some years ago and this couldn't be any tougher. In fact the structure, culture and discipline aspects of the service were based on Royal Navy training and therefore I knew what to expect. Or so I thought.

I'm not sure if it was the fact that I had been overconfident in my ability and resilience at the age of twenty four or if the intervening years had left me with bad habits and a lack of respect for what was about to hit me, but it certainly hit me.

Twelve weeks of being verbally abused, hammered both physically and mentally and never quite sure if I would make the grade. I think my obsessive nature was an advantage and for once a positive trait. Without it I doubt very much if I would have seen the day of the passing out parade. In many ways there was little opportunity for severe intrusive thoughts to enter my conscious mind for the majority of the time and the manner in which I was able to focus intensely on the academic and physical aspects was my saviour. The fear of failure was with me every single day of the course and whilst many others fell by the wayside I battled through, dealing a blow for mental illness.

The weeks passed with examinations every Friday morning and results in the afternoon and if you were lucky a veiled, but more often a not-so-veiled, threat of expulsion if you failed to build on your performance week after week. For me the challenge was the ultimate in mental and physical strength as I drove myself to be better than the rest in each discipline to avoid the fate of many of my new-found friends.

The instructors were certainly playing out some personal vendettas and I sensed that inter-brigade political issues had an influence on the chances of success for certain candidates depending on their postcode. With over a third of the fifty starters being despatched to their personal oblivion in the first six weeks of the course it was always going to be a lottery in terms of survival.

I knew that to study fanatically and demonstrate physical strength and stamina at every opportunity would prove my worth, prove my value and surely show these hard-nosed instructors that I was an asset to any Fire and Rescue Service. The trouble is, a number of them were purely and simply bullies who tried their level best to reduce grown men to being fearful and self-doubting 'wannabes'.

Halfway through the course I had been performing well in all areas and had passed every exam with top marks. I had been a front runner in the physical challenges, which were far and above anything I had previously experienced. Just before leaving for home with my county colleagues, a particularly objectionable instructor who was built like the proverbial brick outhouse, walked into my room for the final inspection before departure. He was unable to find any dirt on the surfaces, floor or woodwork, disorder in my cupboards or find fault with my bed pack, which by now was a block of sheets and blankets in perfect harmony, a sharp edged rectangle with perfect symmetry (no surprise there, then). He turned to me before walking out of my room and said, 'Go home and have a good weekend because on Monday I will have you out of here.'

My heart sank and I wondered what all the hard work had been for. They could manipulate and influence to such an extent that I had absolutely no doubt that he would achieve his ambition. I searched for a reason why this man could feel it necessary to make such a statement in the knowledge that it would have such a devastating effect on his target. Perhaps I am wrong and many stronger people would have the strength of character to merely laugh it off, face the challenge with a brave heart and mind and show this man how arrogant, churlish and mean he was being.

Some of the lads later told me that this tough guy had been watching me closely during some of the extremely intense physical exercises, such as log carrying, hose running and gym tests, and fancying himself as a bit of a macho man, he had clearly targeted me to bring me down a peg or two. I must admit I had been making every effort to match him in each exercise and a little more besides, so he may have taken that as a threat to his superiority.

My entire weekend was taken up contemplating my future and starting to plan how I would explain to people that I had failed yet again. I was sorely tempted to throw in the towel because it was inevitable that my fate was sealed. I was going to let down everyone who had been so pleased that I had finally found my true vocation. Strangely, the obsessive and compulsive part of me and feelings of depression were taking a back seat for one of the few times I could remember. Purely and simply, I was miserable, dejected, and lacking all confidence but not depressed.

I don't know why but I sensed the future was about to change for the worse and there was nothing I could do about it. I decided I would return to the training centre and face the same feeling of sickness that welled up in the pit of my stomach every Sunday evening when driving through the camp gates and seeing the imposing, rusting white drill towers. Monday morning came and there was no sign of the Neanderthal, so the day continued with me oblivious to the fact that he had been taken ill and was not expected to return for quite some time. I felt elation and relief and had a renewed belief in my impending success. His apparent serious illness troubled me a little, but not nearly enough. I felt heartless.

The weeks flew by, examination results got better and better, and I felt good about myself. Nagging doubts about how I had managed to stay in the game started to emerge but nevertheless, I had made it to the end. Such an achievement, but I think passing the course was primarily a way of proving something to myself after being so unproductive since leaving school. Success also meant that I could look forward to having a reasonable income and to being in a position to provide for my family at last. Compared to my brief encounter with the boys in blue, this achievement felt like something that would actually inspire me to greater things and provide me with the perfect opportunity to increase my self-esteem. As my second passing out parade approached I couldn't help thinking that something would spoil my optimism but instead, and to my complete surprise, my squad commander announced that I had been selected to receive the 'silver axe' for being the top recruit of the entire intake.

I had done it again, managed to come on top of the pile but I somehow knew that there must have been a travesty somewhere along the way as I could name at least half a dozen more deserving individuals.

Still proud to be in such a positive position and relieved that the pressure was finally over, I began to consider how it would be possible for me to maintain the standards I had set myself. Luck had clearly been on my side throughout the twelve weeks and the fortunate events at the halfway stage and totally unexpected outcome, created something with which I was not familiar: total removal of pressure for the time being. My mind started to play its usual tricks and the grey matter that had been so busy concentrating on studying and worrying, had finally got some free space. The intrusive thoughts that had always been my nemesis, were once again free to wreak havoc at a time when I should have been celebrating and looking forward to the future.

With hindsight I berate myself for being so ungrateful, when I am conscious that so many of those determined and hardworking newly qualified firefighters would have appreciated the 'silver axe' accolade so much more than me. I wasted the chance to enjoy and grow from the experience and as the day of the parade grew nearer, the efforts to make the archaic training centre into a venue fit for expectant friends and family threw up so many opportunities for me to be carried away again in a groundswell of destructive urges. Suffice to say that by the time I was standing on the top of one of the six-storey drill towers, the familiar feelings of nausea and dread were taking their toll. The flat roof was approximately nine feet by nine feet and barely large enough to accommodate a couple of fully kitted rookies.

There were six of us, fifty feet from the ground. We were attempting to secure the canvas backdrop that would disguise these decaying structures as a block of flats. I approached the edge with two of my newfound friends and held the façade in place. My eyes spotted the hard concrete floor below and I winced as I imagined someone falling to their death. I had no personal fear as at that moment I would not have cared either way if I had received a stout shove in the back. My worries were for the others and their precarious position, being vulnerable in the presence of someone as unbalanced as me.

I must have looked strange as I crouched with my eyes tightly shut so that I could block out the sense of being surrounded by these endangered people. The frightening feeling of paralysis in my arms and legs and tingling in my body that pre-empts the danger-stimulated 'urge' that I have become used to, overwhelmed me. Someone asked me to pass them some rope and I pretended not to hear. I was sweating profusely and felt certain that someone would see me shaking as I resisted the thoughts and tried to focus on not having any part of me touch anyone else.

If I had failed I would have seen it as a deliberate attempt to dislodge them so that I could watch them plunge to their deaths. I was tempted to explain that I had a fear of heights and that for the last twelve weeks I had merely been able to battle through, but I remained silent and hoped that no one had noticed my state of inertia. Finally descending the internal cat ladder I recognised that no matter how I chose to deal with the urges, I would always lose, I would always need more and more reassurance that I had committed no wrong.

No longer thinking about the silver axe, no longer feeling pride and satisfaction at my achievements, I lay on my bed in the little room, my mind a blur of past, present and fears for the future. I longed for a silver bullet that would put an end to my personal nightmare. What a way to show my gratitude, but I couldn't help the way I felt. The parade came and went and I felt little pride when presented with my axe. It still sits on my lounge wall, thirty years on, and you can see it when you walk through the front door. My reflection in the polished chrome is that of a man who remains that same person, but he is stronger, wiser and understands so much more.

17. You have been warned.

Despite successes, I couldn't seem to harvest the feelings of self-worth that achievements normally reap and that always troubled me. I had been told on so many occasions by so many people that I would never be satisfied. To some extent it was an accurate appraisal. I often argued that I could be satisfied for a few minutes, sometimes hours and in extreme circumstances a couple of days but then would be quickly overwhelmed with the need to feel that buzz once again. Many would suspect that my lack of contentment was a legacy from my childhood when I had been under severe pressure to please someone, anyone, my dad maybe. How could that be wrong, given my recollections of those far from rewarding early years? But wasn't that really down to me and my personality?

The reflection in the silver axe reminded me of who I was as I pondered for a moment at the front door before leaving for my first operational shift. My excitement and trepidation were in parallel as I sensed what we all feel when we face the unknown: not quite sure that we will meet our or other's expectations. Not quite achieving may have influenced some of my most difficult times but the real task master has always been my own demanding personality, wanting to set the bar too high. The desire to be the best will always lead to disappointment, eventually.

That was the day that I would discover what life had to offer perhaps, if I was lucky, for the next thirty years or so. My first meeting with the 'gaffer' failed to calm my nerves as he derided me for being a 'silver axe man', and cheerfully exclaimed, 'You can fucking forget it if you think it makes you special, son, because this is where the hard work starts. Yes, you did well, but I can assure you, if you don't manage to retain that level of performance you will be in deep shit and won't last long here. The Training Officer will make sure of that.'

His words of encouragement made me realise that I would need to focus more than ever and I immediately set out my plan of action. I would study obsessively, to ensure that the probationary examinations would hold no fear. There were two years of practical and academic assessments ahead of me and I had already had the 'gypsies warning'. I could not afford to fail. To some extent it was what I needed, what I thrived on, but the added pressure could also lead to my downfall. The OCD and depression would need to be managed and at the same time I would have to be a loving father and a worthy husband.

The first few months on the watch were exciting and filled with operational exposure to the extent that I was immediately called a Jonah. So many incidents and barely any time to learn the more mundane aspects of the role. I attended fires and road traffic accidents (now known as road traffic collisions as nothing is an accident, there is always a cause).

I fought fires wearing breathing apparatus, used heavy duty cutting gear to extricate casualties, operated fire pumps and pitched ladders. Such demanding, adrenaline fuelled activities were surely enough to allow me freedom from my mental torment. The regular rush of excitement was therapeutic, even for me. Some of the more traumatic incidents in those early days did sometimes shock me, making me appreciate the fragility of life. But if I am completely honest, despite not wishing harm, I was one of many that craved and fed from the adrenalin rush and the feeling of satisfaction that came from pretending to be a hero.

Hardened firefighters may portray the image that they are never fazed by the events they witness but I am first hand evidence that this façade is nothing more than a defence mechanism. There are many strange characters in all walks of life and there are some exceptions to the norm, but generally the tough exterior is simply for show and purely in the interests of professionalism. Based on my own experiences, aside from the odd few, most of my colleagues have been compassionate, loyal and empathic.

Pressure began to show as my weaknesses began to encroach on aspects of life that I had hoped were no longer vulnerable. My baby son and little girl were what my home life was all about and whilst work commitments sometimes allowed me to escape from obsessional behaviour there were plenty of occasions when I fell into that cycle of despair that by now seemed to be a blueprint for the rest of my life.

This took a turn for the worse when we were woken in the early hours of a night shift in late 1987 to the report of a house fire. The message resonated throughout the dormitory via the public address speakers and prompted an immediate and focused reaction. Even with my limited experience I could feel the nervous energy as everyone leaped from their 'put me up' beds and struggled into clothes and shoes to race to the pole drop. A report at this time of night could only mean one thing: a genuine and more than likely serious house fire with occupiers trapped in the property. In those days smoke alarm ownership was fairly limited, and nationally the number of deaths in house fires remained at an unacceptably high level. You could generally tell if it was a 'goer' based on the time of call and the message relayed over the tannoy by the Fire Control Operator.

During these times I was no longer an obsessive compulsive individual, I was an integral part of the team. My sleep during stand-down periods on nights was always fitful, but several of my colleagues could have slept standing up, which makes the way in which they transitioned from snoring to firing on all cylinders so much more impressive.

Two pumps raced from the station to the address, barely five minutes away, to see flames leaping from the first and second floors of a standard council semi. Both crews dismounted with breathing apparatus (BA) wearers fully kitted and ready to enter the inferno. A young mother in pyjamas was writhing on the kerbside, screaming hysterically whilst being restrained by an ambulance crew who were also trying to treat her injured leg.

She had been one of eight adults and children in the property, seven of whom had escaped the inferno. She had jumped at the last minute from the bedroom window and landed badly, but fortunately for her it had prevented her from re-entering the property in a desperate bid to look for her two-year-old son. Neighbours lining the street shouted and screamed at us to act quickly to rescue the little boy.

The gaffer hastily briefed two teams each consisting of two wearers and they immediately went under air (BA sets supplying clean air), one team to search and fight the fire on the ground floor and the second to search and fight the fire on the first floor. I was number five, the 'gopher' or 'jockey', which meant I was responsible for setting into the fire hydrant and assisting with hose management as the teams gained entry.

Within what seemed like minutes, the flames were no longer issuing from the property and huge volumes of smoke were visible, pouring from broken windows and the open door. I was sent to the rear of the property to see if I could gain entry once the place had vented. Radio messages coming from the crews inside disturbingly confirmed that the child had not been located. Hardly surprising I thought, as to me it appeared that the entire house was gutted and the chances of survival for anyone unlucky enough to remain inside were absolute zero.

Screaming again from the front of the property confirmed that everyone outside was aware that the boy had not been found and I knew that a tragedy had occurred. I managed to force the back door open and entered the kitchen where a small dog was cowering in a pool of fire water. It bolted through the open door as I approached and I turned my attention to the lounge to my right. The room was devastated and as I entered I realised the futility of harbouring any hope.

The breathing apparatus crews were milling in and out and the smoke was clearing rapidly as I could make out the remnants of the settee and an armchair. My eyes focused on a white patch in the centre of the chair and my brain registered almost immediately that it was what was left of a nappy moulded to a tiny body. The poor little soul had tried to hide from the fire in the only way he knew, by curling up face down and burying his head into the once plump seat upholstery.

My heart sank and I sensed the pain and fear that he must have suffered and the agony his family would now be facing. He was roughly the same age as my son and I couldn't remove that thought from my mind; it would haunt me for many years.

Fire investigation identified that the little boy had managed to pick up a lighter from somewhere and had somehow ignited an item of furniture. Smokers in the home had perhaps not considered the risk and had been unwitting accomplices in this awful tragedy.

This occasion remains the most troubling incident of my career and it had a profound effect on my thought processes, for a number of reasons. I had a son of the same age, I was a smoker, I knew fire, the risks and precautions to take to prevent it, but could I provide the safety my children needed? Would I create the circumstances that would spell danger, would I put my children at risk by carelessly discarding cigarette ends, would I deliberately leave for night duty and not properly extinguish my last smoke? Wouldn't the sensible thing be to simply quit the habit? Wouldn't any normal rational person realise that these fears were self-induced and therefore my knowledge should convince me that my thoughts were nothing more than that? I was predisposed to taking every precaution to avoid feeling that I had caused harm, and that is all well and good with a normal brain. I didn't possess a normal brain.

The madness has never been allowed to undermine my professional judgment, well not that I can recall anyway. This is fortunate and seemingly uncanny given the crippling effect I have suffered at the hands of this illness. Truthfully, it has been difficult on occasions because my sensitivity to the potential for harm remains the same in every aspect of my life but I think due to a combination of self-preservation, determination and pure luck I have been able to separate home and work at least at the more troubling end of my OCD spectrum. Suffice to say that the reason my problems are multiplied when involving my family is largely down to the love I have for them and I suspect that without this love, the OCD would wield less power until it discovered another weakness to feed upon.

18. No time to live.

Life was becoming an increasingly impossible place to be as I struggled with a wide range of concerns, all equally damaging, at a time when my brain could have done with some respite. Respite that would allow me to relax and enjoy my new job, my family and a future that could promise so much.

Firstly, I had two young children who needed twenty-four-hour protection from all the things most people take for granted as being completely safe when managed with a little common sense. Examples would be plug sockets, poking things therein, fluff and everyday household floor debris, sharp corners, blunt corners, hot irons, steam from kettles, cleaning fluids, medicines, knives, forks, food and air itself. These things all had the potential for harm and I was responsible for every single threat.

The simple thing would have been for me to ignore these concerns like any normal person, but that would have been the same as actually wanting the harm to occur. Let's say I didn't pick up the fluff from the carpet, I may as well have fed it directly into the child's mouth. Supposing I saw the child toddle towards the blunt object and failed to dash to the rescue, I may as well have pushed the blunt object into the child's head. Not having bothered to check the cupboard door multiple times, the opportunity to drink the bleach had surely been invited by my irresponsible behaviour. The knife on the worktop, facing in the wrong direction could have fallen and stabbed the child and I had not taken the opportunity to move it, turn it around or permanently track the child.

The growth of these and many more home-based concerns failed to prevent the return of the nasty thoughts whenever I found myself alone with the children. I simply had never done enough, never quite achieved the gold standard and because I failed to demonstrate perfection, it surely meant that I had some underlying desire to cause serious harm. Sometimes I could fight that feeling for weeks at a time and maybe survive without falling into that familiar downward spiral. On the other hand I could easily succumb to the torment and find myself virtually unable to function.

Secondly, the smoking, an ever-present relief valve but a constant threat, presented the next hurdle. Some days it proved to be the perfect cure, a minute or two to walk away and forget the thoughts that poisoned my mind, a period of reflection and on occasions a solution or temporary fix to my dilemma. More often than not I walked back into the house without ensuring the toxic and carcinogenic ash had been removed from my clothing, from my lips, from my hair, from my brown-stained fingers. That was an obvious attempt to harm the vulnerable and I could have spent many hours convincing myself that I had not deposited burning ash inside the home before leaving for work in some devious plan to ensure the house went up in smoke along with the occupants.

This would only become 'merely a thought' once I had ritualistically conducted the safety checks. My roll up had to be extinguished by stubbing repeatedly into the ashtray, always ending up with ash caking my fingers due to the fervent nature of my efforts. I had to lick my fingers to remove the ash, because a walk to the sink to wash would risk dropping the lethal residue on to the carpet or worse still, on to a child. I needed to study my fingers and repeat the chant about how they were clean and I made sure my clothes were checked by a responsible person. If I was not leaving the house, these rituals would not be necessary because I could avoid any future disaster.

Whilst at work I could smoke without fear because how could I behave in the same way when I was surrounded by so many normal people? They would have thought I was mad if I had licked the ash off my fingers. I can't say I would have blamed them either but on the odd occasion where my protective nature influenced me to behave inappropriately I was fortunate enough to have avoided the spotlight and perhaps some questions that would have proved difficult to answer.

Thirdly, the studying. So much of it, hard, intense and for me an absolute necessity to come out on top. After all, I had been given the ultimatum to produce an even higher standard or face the consequences. I had hoped that this significant change to my daily routine would break the cycle of obsession and result in a completely new focus for me. It definitely added a certain something but to say it was entirely beneficial would be foolish. The way my brain worked meant that it provided a level of pressure that left less room for the other baggage, temporarily that is. I called it studying for success whilst learning by obsession.

Finally, I was still able to find time for the old favourites, the washing and cleaning to avoid contaminating others, switching on and switching off to make sure things were properly isolated, opening and closing doors to make sure they were fully closed in case of fire and oh, something I nearly forgot, personal safety. This usually involved the germs on toilet seats and door handles, taps and eating utensils. The list was endless. I think I inherited the entire range of OCD quirks. Eventually it wears you down.

19. New son.

Being in a room alone with people had often prompted weird and starkly disturbing images in my mind but following the birth of my first son, the thoughts became more frequent and more damaging. With two children to look after, my only concern was to occupy them with fun things and allow myself the pleasure of fatherhood. One child alone, however, and almost instantly my mind would introduce destructive elements.

These elements never failed to starve me of loving feelings and threatened my ultimate downfall, sickening me with the belief that I was some kind of monster. I never knew how I would deliver such acts of violence toward my loved ones; it was merely a thought and an immediate internal reaction that left me distraught. The awful fear that I wanted to physically attack was the first step in measuring my loyalty and my ability to protect. I would move towards the victim with a predetermined script of, 'Go on then, just do it'. Although not aware of the proposed act or outcome, I was able to prove my undying love and to congratulate myself on once again beating the curse. Gradually the structure of the 'episodes' made the search for evidence all the more difficult.

The pressure generated by a lifetime of obsessional behaviour was beginning to create neurological overload and I knew of nothing that would halt the process and the downward spiral continued. I think I sensed that 'rock bottom' was on its way. Just moments alone with a child, an adult, anyone, all fostered the same scenario except that as time progressed, weapons entered the arena, making the trial all the more difficult. I saw a bread knife. Did I want to use it? No, of course not, but there was no way of proving it to myself unless I physically grasped it and held it near to the chosen victim.

Sickened, disgusted and saddened by my vile intentions I would be relieved that I had passed the test but what if I had held it there a little longer, what if I had blanked my mind off? The questions came thick and fast in an endless barrage of rapid fire. There was no way out of this: I was wedged fast in a revolving door that would not eject me to open space. But ultimately nothing ever happened. That alone was not enough to prove my innocence.

When I felt a momentary surge of pride for surviving yet another trial by mental torture, someone would enter the room. That single, coincidental interruption would always be a spoiler. How could that be? That person may have been the sole reason for my behaving in a rational way, they may have just saved the child's life. I couldn't get the idea out of my head that someone walking in at that opportune moment may have been the difference between life and death.

This would be another hurdle that I would face on every occasion these battles took place in my brain. Not only was I facing the threat of murderous intent, I was also racing against the clock and, depending on the timing, it could be a good day or a tremendously bad one.

I faced these demons on a daily basis for many months and decided that the only way to cope with this and all the other horrible scenes that played out in my head, would be to spend as little time as possible at home. With that in mind I began to work as often as I could during my days off, using the excuse that the extra money would come in handy to pay for holidays and special things.

I agreed to help a local builder who had previously asked many times if I could spare him some time doing general building work. He made a tidy living buying, renovating and selling property during the eighties and nineties and my somewhat rugged skills as a bricklayer and roofer stood me in good stead for as much work as I could handle. The fact that I was still a human JCB also had a lot to do with his desire to employ me. Having taken the plunge despite the pressures of my real job, studying, family life and the forensic attention to keeping the kids safe against the ever powerful will of my evil mind, I somehow still believed it would be the answer to my increasing desperation.

By the time I completed my second probation examination, I was finding it difficult to fulfil all of my obligations and found that each and every aspect of my life was being suffocated under an enormous cloud of depression and self-loathing. The point of no return had arrived.

People around me were still completely unaware of my mental state and as such were unable to advise me. I had wanted to cope alone and work out for myself how I would defeat this spiteful and aggressive illness. I finally relented, gave in and made an appointment with my GP.

Having not visited the surgery before, I soon found myself explaining why I felt so desperate. Not wanting to feel that I was hiding from my evil thoughts, it all came flooding out and I knew she would probably call the police and tell them I needed to be locked away for a very long time. She didn't; she remained calm and showed sympathy and concern. I was amazed, convinced the story she had listened to would be featured in some volume of psychiatry indicating that this individual represented a severe threat to the community, a ticking time bomb just waiting for the right circumstances to go off.

The diagnosis was clinical depression due to severe intrusive thoughts along with obsessional, compulsive and ritualistic tendencies. She prescribed a course of anti-depressant tablets, starting with a low dose to avoid the immediate onset of side effects and in two weeks' time the dose would be increased as necessary. I left the surgery and raced to the chemists to collect my happy pills. I hoped these little, colourful capsules would be the answer to my dreams.

They absolutely were not, I was too far gone. They failed to even scratch the surface and as I sank to a place somewhere in the earth's core, I was desperate for some unseen force to take me away from this life.

20. The day came.

I began to find it even more difficult to cope with all the things that had been overloading my brain for months. During waking hours and also during troubled sleep, my head was rammed to the point of bursting with the ritual cleaning, washing, checking, reciting and confirming. I lived in fear of becoming something worse than evil involving the children because of not trying hard enough to protect them. The destructive intrusive thoughts continued to eat away at me, loosening my fragile grip on reality. The intensive studying, every spare moment spent repeating and testing and the ever increasing time spent earning that 'extra bit of money for holidays and special things' pushed me to the brink. My brain couldn't take any more.

Waking with that all too familiar sense of dread, anticipating another battle with my renegade brain and its bubbling cauldron of chemicals triggering thoughts of impending doom and gloom felt like an impossible burden. Feeling mildly nauseous as usual and unable to eat or drink, I left the house to spend the day repairing a garden wall for the builder whilst he made himself busy inside the property. Cold and damp, chiselling out and replacing bricks whilst teetering on a cramped and hastily erected platform, my mind drifted to previous moments during my working relationship with the man who by this time felt something of a surrogate father.

I had been working with him for several months carrying out numerous tasks ranging from demolishing walls, fitting lintels, rendering and skimming walls, concreting floors and re-roofing to more mundane activities such as sanding woodwork and painting. The satisfaction I was able to achieve from the more physical aspects goes without saying whilst some of the less challenging tasks with low physical and mental activity stimulated less favourable reactions.

I would spend long periods pondering recent troubling thought processes, analyse my original actions and responses to those thought processes and try to establish a reasonable solution in my head. Sometimes the situations on which I focused were less recent and it could take hours to reach a point where my brain would finally accept the outcome and be comfortable that I had done the right thing. Looking back, these were pointless experiments and in reality I had been leaving myself to the mercy of my brain which would always ambush me at a critical point and force me to start all over again. I would re-enact difficult episodes whilst talking myself through each painstaking step, always conscious that my employer could witness this strange behaviour at any point, merely by arriving at my shoulder without warning.

How I was ever able to complete my work is now difficult to comprehend but I always managed to deliver to his specification and in return he treated me well. Because the pay was extremely poor and over the years I must have saved him a fortune in not having to hire expensive equipment or employ specialist contractors, his manner with me was exceptional, and for that reason I became very fond of him. In return I was occupied, challenged physically and didn't have to face life as a family man or, more accurately, face my responsibilities as a father.

Tools of the trade became extremely important and I knew at the start of every day if there was potential for further anxiety where certain jobs were planned. Sanders and paintbrushes were safe but hammers and saws, chisels and bladed items were not. Working on the roof was safe as he was not particularly fond of scaling ladders or happy with heights. No risk of coming into contact in such lofty environments, particularly as the idea of scaffolding to provide for my safety was out of the question. In fairness I was more than comfortable without such safety precautions, after all, it created greater risk for me to consider and by design took my mind off the other stuff.

Many times, as is my tendency, my focus became the tool that was being held in my hand and eventually even the most innocuous of items became a lethal weapon, because whatever you say about OCD, it's extremely resourceful and progressively more ingenious.

A pencil sharpened with a Stanley knife can become a dagger with the potential for wreaking havoc if rammed into a man's eye or ear or through his temple. Why bother when you have a knife in your hand, a knife that could slice through a man's throat with little or no effort? But that would be too obvious, I couldn't possibly do that, the thought simply makes my skin crawl with disgust. The pencil now; that's a different matter altogether.

Whilst stripping the roof, the sharp, projectile-like slates occasionally fell to the ground and missed the refuse skip which has been strategically placed to collect the debris. He must have been lucky walking beneath the ladder as I deliberately attempted to decapitate him like those poor, unfortunate headless chickens that my old man had targeted. This was so much worse though because he was a human being, and yet oblivious to the crazy mind of the likeable young man on the roof.

The screwdriver in my hand for removing the door was a puncture wound waiting to happen. I had to turn away as he approached, to make sure that it was kept away from his body. A slight brush past could have caused a stumble and then where would we have been? A middle-aged man with a screwdriver embedded somewhere in the ample, over-nourished and whisky-enhanced bulge above his belt.

He walked into the back garden at the rear of the two-up, two-down terrace where he found me mixing concrete by hand to save him having to spend money on an electric mixer. My time was far cheaper than such expenditure and I was almost as effective. The work had given me a feeling of great satisfaction as I completed the final mix for a new floor in the kitchen of the property.

Suddenly and without warning I thought about what would happen if I hit him on the head with the shovel or, worse still, swung the sharp blade towards his neck. I was not initially shocked with these thoughts as they mirrored numerous similar episodes but this was different as I rarely created such vicious temptations when my exertions had served their purpose in creating the usual feel-good vibes. Was this a further sign that things were really getting out of hand?

The repetitive hammer and chisel tune was failing to stimulate my overactive brain and the void was filled with one huge knot of negativity. The builder had stacked a bonfire from the huge pile of rotten skirting, doors and door frames, kitchen units and other combustible items. The fire was burning brightly a few metres behind me, providing a little residual warmth as protection against the cold air.

Frequently appearing through the kitchen door with armfuls of timber, he loaded up the fire and offered pleasantries on each trip. Finally recognising that his fire was almost at the point where a call to my colleagues may have been on the cards, he conceded that it might be a good time to help with the brick cleaning instead. He set to work alongside the rickety home-made scaffold whilst I continued with the task of making good the old garden wall.

Company was the last thing I needed at a time when I had decided that a further visit to the doctor was inevitable. Two weeks had elapsed since my last visit and the notion of suicide was becoming rather more appealing. My take on life was that if the opportunity to simply fall asleep and drift away into oblivion became a reality, I would embrace it and relish the freedom it offered. If only it were that easy.

The bonfire burned fiercely several metres away as I attempted to make polite conversation with my new builder's mate. He chatted cheerfully as he chipped away at the reclaimed bricks purchased from the local merchant, removing the old soft mortar and placing them neatly beside me.

I thumped the two-pound lump hammer hard against the bolster chisel to free the damaged bricks from the wall. Laying the freshly cleaned bricks felt strangely therapeutic, almost as if I was giving the wall a new lease of life and for a brief moment I felt a sense of pride but nothing could remove the feeling of desperation that had been growing for so long. Looking down at him as he hunched awkwardly trying to speed up his work task, I could see that he wasn't a natural handyman. In fact he had been a chartered engineer for many years and highly qualified in his field of expertise. Feeling disillusioned with his professional career, he'd decided to cut his losses and invest in a small greengrocery shop, working all hours and by all accounts making a decent living.

The area served by this small convenience store was somewhat socially deprived and after several burglaries and some random vandalism, he felt the need to sell up, particularly as the property market was fairly buoyant. Turning his hand to house renovation was an unlikely route, but despite his propensity to cut corners and do things on the cheap he became fairly successful. He purchased properties at a low price, spent sparingly to produce a modern feel and always made a hefty profit. Properties were either sold on quickly or retained to add to his portfolio. He could have afforded to pay me the going rate but his argument was that I already had a good income from my proper job and this was a little bit on the side, cash in hand, no questions asked. It was money for special things, those little extras in life.

Without inviting the thought I began to obsess about his safety and the possibility of dislodging a brick, watching it tumble over the edge of the planked platform only to bounce off his neatly combed fifties quiff before hitting the floor. Then almost as if it were a natural progression of that initial fear I saw myself looking at the heavy object in my right hand. His vulnerability struck me and immediately my brain chemicals failed me once again as I looked down at the top of his head. Drained by the months of fighting this dreadful curse, months of self-destructive, obsessional behaviour I wondered what would happen if I hit him on the head with the hammer. Horrified and sickened, experiencing the familiar paralysis in my limbs, I recoiled at the thought. I think I actually made a sound as I mumbled, 'No.'

He looked up as if to ask me what I had said and I turned away to face the wall. My mind told me that the only reason I hadn't struck out with the hammer was that he had chosen that particular moment to look me in the eye. What if he hadn't turned my way, would I have committed that horrific act, inflicting a grievous or fatal injury?

The only way to solve the mystery was to wait until he returned to his original position, then I could prove my innocence and confirm that I was an honourable and harmless human being. I waited nervously, dreading the possibility that he may walk away and get on with another job, thus depriving me of my chance to claim immunity. The opportunity arose and I raised the hammer above his head, barely able to maintain the silence the experiment would require. If he looked now, my fate would be sealed and he would think I was a killer. *Quickly*, urged my brain, *go on, just do it, then.*

I returned the hammer to the plank at my feet and though still feeling nauseous, brow beaded with sweat and body shaking, I knew for a few seconds that I had beaten it this time. But it didn't last and whilst he remained in position I needed to check again and again. On each occasion I cleared my conscience, I redeemed myself, but it was not enough. I knew it would never be enough but I had to try. Because that is what I had to do. That is what I have always needed to do, ever since I can remember. This was different, though, as I usually confined this ridiculous ritual to my closest and dearest because I loved them and because I needed to know how much. Why had I let it go this far?

He stood up and told me he needed to collect some more wood to keep the fire burning and I felt devastated. I worried intensely as I was not satisfied with the outcome of my test, I hadn't proved anything. There was absolutely no doubt in my broken mind that I would have carried out that terrible act if circumstances had been different. Why didn't I get the opportunity to test myself just one more time? I would have felt better. Whereas I simply felt distraught, disgusted and evil.

He left me stewing, and must have noticed I was motionless on the rickety platform, but he said nothing. He disappeared into the little house and I wearily climbed down and walked toward the blazing fire. I stared directly into the flames and felt their warmth and power as the bright colours danced in front of my tearful eyes. I wanted to die and I wanted to die immediately. Fire was a fitting end, poignant, appropriate and final. What about my lovely children, how would they feel when they were old enough to realise that their dad was weak and cared too little to fight for them? It would be painful but I could justify that. The best way to honour my children would be to rid them of me. They would understand that I did it for them.

I held my breath and closed my eyes.

21. The asylum.

How could that huge Victorian structure be so welcoming, so familiar to me despite not having set eyes on it previously? Was it because it was in stark contrast to my suburban semi, comfortable and warm? Was it because it had featured in my dreams over many years, dreams that failed to present themselves in the cold light of day? The four floors of red brick walls, barred windows and enormous chimneys reaching up into the gloomy night air had a kind of soothing effect on me. Gigantic, monolithic, Dickensian, all of these words sprang to mind as I imagined someone like Jack the Ripper had been here before me and a pipe-smoking detective had searched the darkness within for some mad deluded criminal who had sought refuge after committing horrendous crimes.

We'd talked about the nut house as kids, and it represented a place where the weirdest of creatures were incarcerated because they were a danger to society, and were usually mad axemen, cannibals or screaming lunatics. They had to be shackled to their beds in windowless rooms with padded walls and spongy floors to stop them banging their heads until they ran out of energy. Then they would sleep and be injected with drugs to make them sleep even more. Dad had told me about the loony bin, it was a standing joke amongst the normal people in society and anyone that knew an inmate kept it quiet for fear of guilt by association.

The builder had been my saviour some five hours earlier as he appeared from the little house, his arms full of fuel for the fire. He saw me standing silently, gazing into the flames as they licked at the air in front of my face and he knew something was wrong. The familiar, cheerful shape of his faithful employee had been replaced by a man wearing a mask of grey, his shoulders slumped in resignation and unable to utter a word.

He asked if I was OK and I shook my head, tears rolling down my cheeks. He looked into my eyes and realised that I was gone. Grasping me by the shoulder and tenderly moving me away from the heat, he supported me as we walked the short distance to his car, trying to make conversation and at the same time figuring out what to do next. Never having dealt with a situation of this nature he decided to take me home. I found out much later that my other half at the time had warned him of my fragile state and he was, at least in part, prepared for some kind of episode.

Turning into the driveway I refused to get out of the car and urged him to take me away, to take me anywhere to avoid having to face the terror of confronting my greatest fears. I had failed in extraordinary circumstances and I would surely fail in familiar ones.

Two hours later the surgery allowed me in without an appointment, my GP still at her desk despite the late hour and the practice being officially closed. I begged her to lock me up, expressing my desire to protect all that was dear to me. She initially wanted to increase my medication, to avoid a knee jerk reaction but I think she understood my fear and didn't want to increase the anxiety, recognising as I had, that it would surely take too long to influence the chemicals in that critical area of my brain. The chances of short-term benefit were slim but the possibility of short-term catastrophe was too much for me to contemplate. I begged again to be admitted to a psychiatric ward because I had spent too long living in doubt and dwelling on so many worst case scenarios. She quickly made the arrangements by telephone and here I was, relieved and safe at last.

Walking into the building, the urge to end my life was once again extremely powerful, but I had already been lucky today with the pressure valve activating before I had taken the final step. I had arrived at a point where a sense of reason had allowed me to believe it was not my time. I craved normality and to be able to feel like everyone else around me rather than a nomad drifting aimlessly, with no hope amidst a crumbling existence. Perhaps I should give more credit to the builder and less to some form of last minute rational thinking.

They let me in and looked at me with sympathy but also with a wary eye, as if they were not quite sure if I would suddenly shriek abuse and lunge for their throats. My chaperone (the builder) explained that I had self-referred and it seemed to create an air of relaxation as I was obviously not as mad as other unfortunates, who had to be carried kicking and screaming to the secure unit.

I know what we can do; we can pump this rather small fellow full of drugs because he has severe OCD and chronic clinical depression. We must take this precaution as there is a distinct possibility that he will self-harm, indeed he has admitted that he would like to end his life.

My brain recalled a recent conversation with my GP regarding this particular drug of choice and my previous reaction to it. Fleetingly, I considered repeating my thoughts out loud. I decided against it as I realised that they obviously knew best. I accepted the tablets and the world soon became calm and white. That didn't last. The sickness in my head multiplied tenfold during the next twenty four hours and everything became blacker than I could have ever imagined.

I was hit by a strange flashback from when I was approximately four years of age. So, there was life before nine, after all. We were all down at the brook in the village, Dad fishing, and Mum, three sisters and me, sitting in the sunshine having a picnic of jam sandwiches and orange squash. Flies were dive bombing the food, too close for comfort because of the cow pats nearby.

Dad called me over to the edge of the brook which opened out into a small pool, probably about thirty feet from one side to the other. It looked deep and I couldn't swim. Dad thought I could do with some life experience to help me toughen up. I was far too sensitive to be a boy so he often tried to instil that rough, tough mentality that he and his five brothers had needed to build in order to survive. He picked me up and threw me in. I think there may have been some comment along the lines of, 'Kids learn to swim if you chuck them into deep water, it's an automatic response.'

It may be an automatic response when a newborn is delivered in water or when a baby is offered the opportunity to survive underwater for a few seconds but not so true for a petrified four-year-old. Not this four-year-old anyway as I immediately started to sink.

There is a vivid memory of looking up and seeing the surface move away whilst I struggled to the surface once, or twice maybe, just in time I think to catch a glimpse of Dad, and Mum shouting at him as he kicked off his shoes. I went below the surface once more and it felt almost peaceful, tranquil; I saw some flashes and I imagined I could see the sun shining and then nothing. Looking back over the years I have wondered if those flashes had something to do with my life and transition into death. Next I saw myself back on the grass bank and I couldn't honestly say how I got there but I do recall Mum crying. Dad was a hero as he had plunged in to rescue me. Maybe he had underestimated the depth of the water, but I think he genuinely believed I would swim.

My brain is telling me that he felt no guilt and I didn't think for a moment that he wanted to kill me, but perhaps this was the start of insecurities that resulted in escalation of my personal frailties. Could this event have been the catalyst for a change in my character or were the foundations already laid? From the moment I left the womb was everything past and present and everything yet to happen written in my DNA? My vulnerability, the chemical imbalance, my mortality and the path I must follow, rubber-stamped by a biological roadmap?

There was friendly and sympathetic support on the ward, and the smiling Sri Lankan lady was my psychiatrist. She surely made a mental note that I had mentioned my previous bad reaction to the proposed medication and that I 'never wanted to feel like that again'.

What part of 'reacted badly' did they not understand? I assumed they just didn't believe me and they also knew that in there, I was no longer in control of my own destiny. Decisions would be made for me over the next few weeks and if I spoke out or behaved in a manner that identified my mental fragility, I could expect more of the same. I was a twenty-seven-year-old family man, with two young children and a respectable career. Two young children who wouldn't understand when they visited that their daddy was more secure here, he felt safer and the kind people, the helpers in normal clothes rather than hospital uniforms, had to make sure he didn't hurt himself.

There were many sad things happening in this place and night time was the worst with the middle-aged man shouting out, 'Mummy, Mummy!' for hours on end and the ramblings of my neighbouring dementia sufferer, but at least the kids wouldn't get to witness it.

When I dared to speak up about the extreme anguish I had experienced because of that initial drug infusion, it was made clear to me that I was not a reliable witness and that I shouldn't worry as these things happened sometimes and it would get better in time. The fear that this would happen again was so intense that I felt I could actually taste it, anticipate the pain. But I knew they knew best, so what was the point of complaining? Never mind, I only agreed to two weeks in here and after that I would be free again, fully recovered and ready to take on the world once more. Two weeks? At that moment I was not so sure what I agreed to and who knew what they would decide to do with me? Perhaps I had made a huge mistake and they would never let me out.

22. ECT (Electro Cardiac Therapy): is it my miracle?

Doug was more than twice my age and had obviously had a hard life because his face told a thousand stories of hardship and sadness. He was worried and tried to put on a brave face for my benefit. He also knew that the next course of electric shock treatment would do the trick. He had been exposed to this innovative solution twice before and although it had destroyed him mentally in the days following treatment, the memory had faded and there was always the chance that it would stop him living in the past and remember that the bereavement pain he had suffered was only short term and he would start to feel better.

'The doctors know best,' he told me. 'And I need to try something because my life is not worth living at the moment. My wife was everything to me and she suddenly left me to cope on my own and I don't know how to do that. I would like to call it a day but I will just take my teeth out again and lie on the table. See you when I recover enough to speak in two or three days! When my daughter comes in later will you tell her that I love her?'

The trip to the other side of the hospital must have been an ordeal for Doug, but clearly one that he was prepared to face. His demons were so debilitating that he was unable to function in the outside world despite the support of his remaining family. I knew his burden was as significant to him as mine to me, but it troubled me. If he was struggling to cope with bereavement and suffered so badly, how could my own self-inflicted troubles have any real credence? I felt that I carried all the worries of the world on my shoulders and he was old enough to know that you can get over a bereavement given time, wasn't he? But he was such a nice man that I started to think of reasons why I should feel ashamed to be here, when I needed to show some grit and pull myself together.

Doug appeared the next day but I didn't see him; all I saw was a shell of a man who didn't recognise me and was unable to speak. His face was grey and he shuffled into the dormitory, supported by two members of staff. He looked at the floor as dribble crept from the corner of his mouth. His eyes had lost their shine, appeared to be smaller, and had receded into deep, dark sockets. With dead eyes and lids flickering, he was laid on his bed. I watched for a few seconds as his arms and legs noticeably shook.

The staff ushered me into the day room where I began to consider my chances of having the same treatment. If it didn't work, why would I care as I probably wouldn't know anyway? If it did work and for that level of distress, the chances had to be good otherwise the experts wouldn't allow it, I would be saved.

I decided to wait until Doug felt better when I could talk to him properly to discover what he really thought about the treatment. He would be more qualified to give me an honest opinion having just faced the ordeal and he would tell me if it was worth the pain, if it had helped him come to terms with life or ultimately made him realise that he, too, would never be free.

Doug didn't get back to normal; he was distant and sad and said very little to anyone. The experts thought he had improved but I sensed he was dying inside. He was discharged within a few days and I lost the opportunity to speak to him. I wanted to know why they had let him go when he was so different to the man that had shared his reasons for sadness with me so openly a while ago. The nice nurse, the young one whom I found quite attractive said, 'Don't worry about Doug, he has been through this before and there will be a marked improvement over time. There are no guarantees but it does work for some.'

I decided to bite the bullet and get it off my chest. 'Can I have the treatment, because I would like to wake up and not feel the way I do?'

She replied immediately, 'Sorry, Oliver, it is not something we would recommend for your condition.'

23. Bedlam.

I recently watched a TV programme that investigated the history of these places built by the Victorians and their association with modern-day celebrities. My own small amount of research informed me that the first recorded 'Lunatic Asylum' in Europe was Bethlem Royal Hospital in London (otherwise known as Bedlam). The building was originally constructed in 1247 as a priory, and mentally ill patients were first admitted in the early fifteenth century. Prior to the 'Madhouses Act' in 1774 the proprietors of such establishments were in it for the money, having little or no concern for the patients. The County Asylum Lunacy Act of 1845 was the precursor to the construction of asylums in every county. Some one hundred or more were completed and stocked with unwilling residents and although the official view was that those unfortunate enough to spend time in such institutes were patients rather than prisoners, these stark and grimly unwelcoming places were not highly regarded for the level of care provided. Privacy was rare, daily routines were strict and regimented and wards were all under lock and key. The ailments or sometimes extremely unfortunate circumstances that led to an individual being accommodated within, could often result in a lifetime of incarceration.

Fortunately for me things had moved on a little, I say a little in all seriousness because in my asylum the evidence of Victorian life seemed to echo from all corners. The structure, the décor, the rules and abject despondency all added to an atmosphere that screamed of desperation. You may not know that people used to visit Bedlam for a day out, like a trip to the theatre, to enjoy the strange goings on, to have a laugh.

I became acquainted with a little old man who had been a patient for over fifty years, always busy collecting cigarette butts from ashtrays, bins and the grounds around the site. He would dismantle these with great care and deposit his spoils into his tin for use with his rollups. He seemed happy enough and was apparently well versed in scavenging other commodities too. Rumour had it that he had been sectioned more than fifty years ago because he was one of those difficult individuals; not bad, violent, wicked or strange, more like challenging or disruptive. I suppose we were talking autism or ADHD or something similar but as you know things do get embellished and taken out of context over time. Despite the Chinese whispers, staff were adamant that although he was now well and truly institutionalised, it had not always been so. Very sad. That said, I would put money on the fact that he rarely worried about the risks of smoking or causing fires by carelessly disposing of his hard-earned smokes.

The thought of becoming reliant on this place frightened me and served to make my mind up that after only two weeks I could also become institutionalised. That sounds ridiculous but I guess what I really mean is that I felt safe. I felt extremely unhappy but safe. Perhaps that was good too, but I certainly didn't want to become the little old man. That was quite a poignant reminder for me, as people at work always said I looked old and wrinkly for my age.

At just twenty seven, I worried about that but put it down to banter. I couldn't see it at all, certainly not in the mirror, but the well-documented Fire Service humour decreed that it must be accurate and so who was I to argue? I recall on many occasions being advised to 'go and iron your face'. Don't get me wrong; my early years in the service were wonderful, but you had to take the rough with the smooth. When certain individuals on my shift decided to call me psycho when I returned to work, the humour was completely lost on me, but that is another story. I didn't really feel it was a laughing matter but I laughed just the same. Rewarding careers must have the odd negative to balance things out I suppose.

24. My brain or someone else's voice.

The softly spoken Sri Lankan lady simply asked a lot of the questions my GP had been asking in recent months. Kindness and empathy oozed from her lips and that was reassuring as it was the first time I had ever been assessed by a professional brain doctor. We talked about the mild dose of anti-depressant I had been prescribed and whether in the weeks since commencing the treatment, I had felt any better. Personally I had not seen any improvement in either my OCD symptoms or the depression that had been growing gradually over recent months and the obvious answer was to increase the dose and see what happened. It seemed to me that the Anafranil was making no difference at all but maybe the fact that I was still alive was testimony to the fact that it had been successful, thanks to my GP, who retired within three years. She was a senior partner at my local surgery and was only in her mid-forties. I knew there was something special about her too, because she really understood me. I discovered later that she had suffered with depression throughout her life and it had become so severe that the amount of time she was away from work had become unsustainable and the partners had asked her to leave.

The psychiatrist asked me, 'Oliver, these worries you have and the intrusive thoughts about your children must make you extremely sad. Do you know where these thoughts come from?'

'Yes I know where they come from, they come from inside my head, from my brain, it's almost like my brain wants to put them out there deliberately to make me unhappy and to encourage me to worry more. I have always worried but these thoughts make me feel physically sick and the more I focus on them, the more I worry. The vicious circle is not complete until I lie down on my bed and cover my head with my pillow and cry. This is why I am here now. If I hadn't admitted myself to this place I really think I would have ended it all for good.'

With my fears revealed, my drugs were increased, making me feel like a zombie so that I couldn't function. When family came to visit in the following days, they knew I was different. I was calm and quiet and not demonstrating signs of anxiety, but I wasn't me. I wondered if I had answered that question differently, the one about where the thoughts came from, would I have been locked up indefinitely?

'Oliver, these worries you have and the intrusive thoughts about your children must make you extremely sad. Do you know where these thoughts come from?'

'Oh yes, of course, it's the voices.'

'Voices, what do you mean voices, Oliver?'

'Voices that I cannot control.'

In that scenario my worry would not be that my brain works in strange ways and that the slightly different wiring creates an obsessive compulsive nature, it would be that I knew if I said I heard voices it would mean I was mad, psychopathic or schizophrenic. I would be found out for sure. That's the trouble with OCD, you just cannot win and the moment you reach a positive place and finally some semblance of order, it brings you right back down to earth. The trouble is that you fall harder each time, well, at least in my case, and it seemed to me that hospital made it worse rather than better. I was so relieved that I wasn't sectioned.

Recently I have discovered that the 'do you hear voices' question is a genuine enquiry made by mental health professionals worldwide, even with new mothers facing the trauma of postnatal depression. Some one in ten new mothers suffer from the debilitating effects of this illness and I have heard that the symptoms can sometimes be as extreme as harbouring thoughts of harming the new arrival. Questions like this are therefore not infrequent and I am encouraged by the fact that people experiencing such intrusive thoughts are able to benefit from effective treatment. Nice to think one is not alone; it makes me feel strangely comforted.

25. Free again!

Two weeks residency seemed like an eternity, but I knew that if I could escape for a while I would feel a lot better and more assured that I had at least some kind of future, not needing to rely on this secure haven. Strange, as I was free to leave at any time but it still felt like I was a prisoner. Christmas 1988 was approaching fast and I couldn't bear the thought of spending the holiday period in that desperate place. I swear that the nursing staff had more reason to be treated like prisoners than us and they definitely shouldn't be released to roam freely amongst the public. Maybe that was just my disturbed mind playing tricks on me. The nice young nurse was normal, but she was a student and had probably not experienced enough of life's draining episodes to show signs of wear and tear – yet!

So, it was time to go home for a few days and although it was exactly what I wanted, the mere thought of walking back into the real world after my rest scared the living daylights out of me. You may ask why and to be honest I am not sure now but I think it was that despite my reservations about the mental health system and the archaic conditions to which I had been exposed, it was safe. I was safe and everyone else was safe from me which meant my inability to be able to protect my family was not an issue. No sooner had I left the confines of the grounds, my nerves and fears resurfaced, sending shivers down my spine. My hands became moist while my brain was telling me to call the whole thing off as it would never work and I needed to be protected inside those stark Victorian walls and barred windows once again.

I persevered with the emotions which I felt were close to beating me, and managed to get as far as the driveway to my home. The car was being driven by my father-in-law. He had been a good friend to me during that period and he was able to separate the real me from this shadow of a man that he now saw. The door opened and I immediately saw my little girl and baby son with their mother in the doorway. They spotted me, but I couldn't get out of the car. I was frozen in place and felt that no amount of coaxing was going to get me out of there.

However, under duress I later found myself sitting in the house nursing my son and trying to engage like a daddy should with his enthusiastic daughter. They had visited me in the hospital but that was such an alien environment that it had been difficult for us to behave like a family.

The awful thoughts returned, meaning I had failed miserably with the first stage of my integration back into society. I was immediately escorted back to hospital where it felt safe. Looking back, it is surreal to think that within the space of a few months of realising there was something wrong with me, it had become a challenge to behave like a human being, even with the two people I loved so dearly. I couldn't speak to them, I couldn't look at them and I certainly couldn't look after them. It was very difficult to drive away. I knew it was better that way but at the same time it was a very painful decision. When would I be able to live up to my family's expectations and feel vaguely normal?

26. The little window.

I had spotted the little window as soon as I walked into the cold, stark ward bathroom on the first day. It must have been the only window free from half-inch-thick metal bars and, of course, far too small for anyone to squeeze through. It was four floors from the ground and peering down to the concrete below during that first few hours made me certain that if I ever were in need of an escape route, this was it. What I mean is that if ever I got to the point of desperation, I was small enough and agile enough to use the opening as my last resort. Sixty feet to a solid floor would surely be enough to finish me off. The fear I felt from the thought made me realise that I was in the best place after all.

Fleeting but excruciatingly destructive thoughts were constantly threatening my sanity and on so many occasions the obvious answer was to find the quickest way to end it all to prevent further torture. I never actually noticed the downward spiral and before I did, I always became acutely aware of a thousand ways to end my life. I doubt if all the methods I considered during that period would have actually completed the job, but I am guessing that the damage done would at least have focused my mind on the pain and maybe created a means of banishing the bad thoughts inside me.

The window was so tempting but I later discovered that it wouldn't open wide enough for even me to force my way out for four floors of free fall. I broached the subject with one of the staff on the ward and discovered that a sorry individual who had managed to avoid attention had been able to give it a try and thus spoil the opportunity for everyone else. Clearly inconsiderate and extremely selfish. They never said if the individual managed to fly or if they fell to their death but the window retained its appeal. Thirty years on, I wonder if my dreams created the window or if my wayward brain had stored false memories. The reality is that I know even today I could take you to that exact window.

For some reason, the memory of the window reminds me of an image of a young man with a gentle voice. He was a cheerful soul who had spent a number of periods inside this 'hospital'. He seemed so bright on that first day that I struggled to understand what was wrong. He appeared so normal. Before long, however, I noticed a raised red scar encircling his neck. He had tried to hang himself a few weeks earlier and had been sectioned for his own safety. Sadly, it was not his first serious attempt to end his life, it was one of many. I guess being homosexual in 1987 was even harder than it is nowadays. I often wonder if he later succeeded in his quest. Strangely poignant really as one of my boys recently confessed to being bisexual, but he is happy, successful, and feels totally accepted. In his head he is as good if not better than many, and rightly so. Perhaps society has changed or is it simply genetics that allows us to accept that we are what we are: strong or weak, happy or sad? Is it nature or nurture or just down to the roll of a dice? I wonder which part of the brain decides these things, and if anyone can do anything about it.

I read a book recently, written by a doctor, brilliantly articulated and in such simple language that it provided a real insight into the workings of the brain. He gave reasons for reactive emotional responses, how to manage the conflict between different areas of the brain and their relative power in influencing thought processes and actions. He describes brain functions in simple terms and identifies the three major components as Chimp, Human and Computer[2].

I could relate to this as the Chimp is all that is bad in my brain, driving me in the wrong direction with false perceptions, bullying me with emotional responses and the desire to seek constant reassurance to confirm the most unreasonable standards. My Human brain is the part that has rational thoughts but has failed to manage the Chimp, allowing the emotional side to take control.

I don't take the blame for all of this as my Computer has numerous files of accepted and learned behaviours that act as my default. The way I see it, the three major parts of my brain have lost their way and have never been taught the right way to interact. The Chimp brain is many times stronger than the Human brain and acts far more quickly, overpowering any sensible thoughts and conclusions I manage to reach. The Computer is even quicker to react, but now I understand that I learned so little in my early years that my Computer is packed full of 'the wrong stuff'. When I seek a default answer for my irrational and intrusive thoughts, I am sent up blind alleys. One day I will learn to manage my Chimp!

---

[2] *The Chimp Paradox* by Dr Steve Peters

27. Forbidden territory.

Dad didn't like hospitals, especially not lunatic asylums. There was nothing worse than showing weakness and it was quite obvious that anyone weak enough to want to kill themselves was not worthy. He talked of his younger days and about one of his best friends who had a son with a number of learning difficulties and psychological problems. According to Dad, he was a 'nutter'. There's no wonder I was scared of him finding out that I, too, had succumbed in the same way and would never be anything other than one of those people.

I remember many years ago when I tried to become a boxer; the man with psychological problems was also practising the noble art of pugilism. I didn't know him, but Larry was an unmistakeable figure, extremely tall and gangly. I saw him in the ring for the first time and realised that he was not quite as he seemed and I wondered then why he had been allowed to undertake this brutal path despite having obvious vulnerability.

He couldn't box but had all the gear; someone must have supported him and allowed it to happen. Thirty seconds after the bell, it was over; a devastated and distraught twenty-something struggled forlornly to the dressing room. I was twelve years old and felt sympathy, compassion and concern. These emotions have followed me closely over the years and I think that means I may not be such a bad person.

'That hospital,' Dad had said. 'Why is he in there? I won't go there, what's wrong with him? He needs to pull himself together.'

My old man didn't understand anything to do with the brain. To him it was 'a load of old cobblers', a disease for wimps and odd people, something that didn't happen to strong men. The stigma attached to mental illness at the time was firmly embedded in Dad's psyche and nothing was going to change that, least of all a cry for help from a son that had disappointed from an early age. Those play fights to toughen the lad up had obviously been a waste of time and perhaps he should have been subjected to more extreme tactics.

Surprisingly, and for me slightly regrettably, he turned up at the asylum and walked through the doors with a strange look on his face. I couldn't tell if it was shame or fear. He didn't understand and therefore had always treated mental illness with scornful contempt, much like the majority of society that didn't understand. We sat opposite each other, neither of us quite knowing what to say, breaking the awkward silence with a few pleasantries. Finally, he asked me why I had committed myself to this primitive environment, asked why I hadn't just spoken to him, or anyone. Surely this could have been prevented?

I tried to explain by mentioning a conversation we'd had when I was eleven, but for one thing he couldn't remember and more importantly, he just wouldn't understand. I often ask myself if this was due to his own loveless upbringing where the strongest always managed to come out on top and the weakest faded into obscurity. He made me promise that I would get out of the place quickly. He told me to think about how much I had going for me and that the important thing was my young family and how they would manage without me. Of course I knew this was true and focused my brain on the fact that I was letting a lot of people down. Maybe I just needed to 'get a grip' and earn some respect from everyone rather than hiding away behind this mask of depression.

He left without gaining an insight into my world and I started to feel that he may be right after all. I would give it a few more days and next time the psychiatrist spoke to me I would convince her that I was feeling much better and no longer at risk of harming myself, that it would be good for me and the rest of my family if I went home. I knew that I wasn't ready but sometimes you just need to do things. The key objective was to get home and call Dad to let him know that I had been tough enough to pull myself together and think of my family.

Late on a Thursday evening in January 1988, three weeks after entering the asylum, I telephoned him from home. I must admit, the response from him was better than anything I had ever experienced in terms of fatherly respect. I went to sleep an hour later, relaxed and pleased that for once the old man was happy with something I had done. I would never get to experience a repeat of that momentous occasion. Three hours later we received a panic telephone call from my sister. Dad was dead, passing away half an hour earlier from a massive heart attack at just fifty two years of age.

Many months passed before I was able to come to terms with this event, but now as I approach my fifty-third birthday in fine physical health I realise that I am blessed in some ways and cursed in others, as he was. But at least that final call was one that he needed and in his world had created a sense of achievement as a father, and one that was never to be destroyed by time and possible future disappointments. Thankfully he never knew that the spiral of depression driven by OCD, or perhaps the spiral of OCD driven by depression, would continue to plague me. He never knew that the troughs would get deeper and the occasional peaks would peter out almost as soon as they had arrived.

I had never explained to him that the thoughts I'd had as a child had been eating away at me all these years. I was never able to confide in him that the same intrusive thoughts were part of me and always would be. It would have been pointless anyway because he would not understand that the brain has power way beyond the boundaries of human intelligence.

28. Back to work, life is normal.

I certainly wasn't ready to return to work, but I needed to occupy my time fully, to find sufficient mental stimulation. Work would allow me to focus on adult things and I couldn't risk being away from that environment for much longer. I had fought against a long stay in the asylum and now it was time to face the next stage of my recovery. I was told by everyone – doctors, family and friends – that I should not attempt to rush into an early return as it could be detrimental to my long-term prospects.

I must admit that I felt strong enough to face my work colleagues but I think that was more to do with a refusal to accept the extent of my 'breakdown' rather than a true sense of improvement. It would be many months, even years until I could safely say that I would be firing on all cylinders. I got used to a perception of feeling normal when the truth was quite the opposite. It was like being in denial because I wanted to be seen as the old me, the person that those on the outside once recognised.

The problem is, word soon gets around and to face the reality of life on the outside can be an extremely difficult challenge.

The first day back on shift was one of the hardest things I have ever done. That may sound an exaggeration given some of the things I have been through but feeling like I was under the spotlight and with the constant need for reassurance, I began to doubt my ability to break the cycle and just be myself. I soon became aware that there were so many emerging and evolving crises ready to bring me back to reality with a hefty bump.

There was no doubt that the entire shift knew I had been absent for reasons of a psychological nature and I was more than happy that there would be no need for me to announce my stay as a guest of the mental health system. They had no idea of the cause or extent of my illness but for a small minority the facts were irrelevant. Rumours and insensitive remarks flowed with no apparent regard for the truth. Friends couldn't decide if it was better to tell me what others were saying or to pretend that my return had raised little more than a ripple.

My Sub Officer, 'the gaffer', called me into the station office and gave me the benefit of his experience and knowledge as a counsellor and superior. It was meant to be the standard return to work interview, procedural, a tick in the box and a pleasant welcome back to the fold. It really wasn't like that but was nothing more than I expected.

'You sure you're OK to be here? How long you been off for, three months is it? Anything I can do for you? You've got to pull yourself together now and get on with it because you need to get ready for your next probation examination in three months. Anything you are concerned about, just let me know and I will sort it for you. Don't take any notice if anyone takes the piss, they don't mean it . . . psycho, ha ha ha.'

He definitely meant it as a joke, I understood that, but it made me realise it would be wise to grow a thick protective skin as quickly as possible. This was the point where I came to terms with how my reputation was now shattered and my credibility probably irretrievable.

There were a few people who would choose to remind me again and again of my association with madness but despite never failing to hurt and degrade me, it had a positive effect in terms of how I perceived them and my understanding of the stigma attached to mental illness. I tried to respond with a smile and a sharp riposte, to show that I was no longer a weird individual and that I accepted their humorous remarks as their way of making me feel welcome. Deluded as it may seem, I felt under so much pressure to fit in and to forget the past, that to react in any other way would have been counterproductive.

In truth I genuinely believe that a large part of the 'banter' was simply a sign of the times. How could they not find it difficult to relate to me? They wouldn't know how to handle it. No one did in those days. Now, twenty five years later, they would know, they would have to. I have noticed the striking differences in perception and understanding over the years and having learned so much from those early months, I am sure this is where some of the foundations of my strength were laid. The years have passed and colleagues have come and gone, but rarely have I encountered the bigotry and poison that I faced at that time.

Maybe fifteen years after my return to the station, I visited a fellow mental illness sufferer on the site of the old asylum. Things had moved on fairly rapidly within the local mental health system and a new building had been constructed which was designed to accommodate a variety of conditions but had the capacity to create suitable environments for each. Where I had been treated in a ward housing patients with dementia, psychosis, drug and alcohol addiction, personality disorders and nervous afflictions, Pete was amongst similar sufferers relaxing in cosy, home-like facilities more in keeping with modern standards and, more importantly, offering supported rehabilitation.

Gone were the filthy dormitories with mouldy green and off-yellow silk-painted walls. Gone were the barred windows and locked doors, slop for lunch and regimented routines. The level of respect afforded to patients was in stark contrast with my own experience and was real evidence of the increased investment in providing for mental health services.

Pete was also a 'silver axe' man but had joined the job a few years before me. Previously excelling in his early career as a bricklayer, competing and placing in national competitions, he found the transition to fire service life easy. He completed all statutory promotion exams within two years. He had no aspirations for promotion but enjoyed the challenge.

His apparent fall from hero to zero occurred quickly and without warning, at least to those who worked with him. I guess his family knew about his darker side but, as with most sufferers, little evidence escaped the inner being until it was too late. Pete never returned to work after almost twenty years service and his seemingly unexpected descent into desperate times. He had a young family and inexplicably had attempted to end his life by trying to battle with the crusher in the back of a refuse lorry.

We never talked about this specifically but chatted at length about the tragedy of mental illness and the lack of understanding by the general population. We talked about hiding the inner self, and the struggle to maintain the outward persona that wears the smile. He was heavily medicated at the time but I remember we agreed on some simple truths. You never know when it will happen and you never know who will be the next one to fall but that fine line is always there, waiting to be crossed. We haven't spoken for a few years now but I will always admire him for battling through and holding on to his life and his family. He made me see that maybe, just maybe, I wasn't as unfortunate as I imagined.

Pete and I had something other than the silver axes in common. Scientists seem to be pretty sure that intelligent people may be more susceptible to mental illness. This is sometimes considered to be a characteristic of people suffering from disorders such as bi-polar disorder and schizophrenia. I am happy with a similar distinction if it raises my profile a little but I tend to think it's a combination of many things. Could it be that greater intelligence encourages greater analysis, increased mental activity and a more intense emotional state of mind?

29. Mr Punch.

Never retaliating, and smiling as often as possible, I managed to ride out the storm of those early months. Resounding success in my final probation assessment gave me the confidence to try and look to the future with optimism. The first year or so was extremely hard as the OCD stubbornly refused to soften and as a result the depression remained a constant threat. Medication was an important factor in my recovery and after several months of reducing and increasing the dose to find a level at which I could function, I settled on slightly more than my GP had prescribed originally. I was showing few outward signs of anxiety and could manage day to day without being totally debilitated.

Too many milligrams and the side effects created a zombie who could trip over a shadow, too few and I was unable to face the day because of an overwhelming urge to surrender to my obsessional behaviour. My body, now familiar with the chemical infusion it had previously found unhelpful, had become saturated and the balance was about right. I awoke every morning with the same awful thoughts, gloomy outlook and fears for the day ahead but more often than not, found the strength to give it a try.

The gaffer had mellowed slightly and had become bored with the little jokes, choosing to focus on one of the other lads for the time being. Character flaws, physical features that stood out, anything that could be considered different was fair game in that testosterone-fuelled environment. Ground rules relating to equality, bullying, harassment and core values were irrelevant in those days and you could say anything to anybody without fear of recrimination.

Some years later, he was unfortunate enough to suffer from a stress-related illness and spent many weeks away from work. I felt no satisfaction at the time but could not help thinking that maybe he would realise the error of his ways and gain an appreciation of what he had encouraged all those years ago.

Peer pressure, a need to feel part of the group and not being able to raise your head above the parapet for fear of it being shot off, was the culture of the day and few had either the confidence or inclination to challenge the norm. I recall one day when I was showering after a Brigade football match soon after recruitment. I felt a warm sensation rolling down my leg. Looking to my right I observed one of my supervisory managers was peeing down my leg and once my awareness had been noted, roars of laughter and cheers reverberated around the changing rooms.

I stood for a few seconds contemplating my next move and quickly realised I needed to be one of the lads and laugh it off and then I could allow myself to be disgusted later in private. I forced a smile and called him a 'dirty bastard', which received even more laughs and then they moved on to someone else. If he had been aware that I was heading for a breakdown I assume he wouldn't have done it. Having said that, it's not something I would ever dream of doing, but we are all different aren't we?

Nicknames were rife and despite many of them being inappropriate and in poor taste, they were culturally acceptable. Mr Punch was one of these and in many ways quite fitting because of his prominent facial projection. He and I had never been very close but out of a Watch strength of sixteen men (no women in the service at the time) there had to be someone you found less palatable than others. Loud and confident, an 'old sweat' and everyone's joker, he made it no secret that my transgression into abnormality was unforgivable. Psycho was hardly a term of endearment but I had accepted it and as time passed it was used less frequently.

I entered into the fun and games without participating in the less tasteful episodes but on one occasion made the mistake of arguing with the dominant one. This didn't go down well and he was obviously rattled by my misplaced audacity. How dare this proven mentalist challenge his superiority? Rather than walk away I used the Mr Punch handle once too often, He responded with an acerbic, caustic assault where the Psycho word had significantly more impact. It was said with such venomous intent that my sense of reason failed to kick in. You could say that the emotional part of my brain was well and truly unleashed and I am ashamed to say that I launched myself at Mr Punch with a view to teaching him a lesson, but with no idea of how that lesson would be taught.

Maybe the stored emotion from so many supposedly innocent but subconsciously hurtful remarks had resulted in this uncharacteristic response but I held him against the lockers in the kit room, my strength too great and too sudden for the much bigger man to react. No punches were thrown, (no pun intended), but I am sure my words resounded clearly in his brain. He knew never to take advantage of my vulnerability again, and as I watched him slink away without a word I felt no pride in what I had done. Part of me felt guilty, as if somehow I had let myself down, shown myself to be exactly what he had inferred. The more I thought, the more guilt I felt.

Neither he nor anyone else ever again uttered the term Psycho in my presence again, but maybe they should have; maybe I would have felt better. They only stopped because now they were right: it was too risky, you don't call a real psycho, Psycho. For me, getting him off my back wasn't even a hollow victory, it felt like I just couldn't win.

30. Struggling through.

Starting to focus as much as possible on my job in order to sidestep as many helter-skelter descents into endless brain dramas, I discovered an ability to pass promotion exams. Practical and theoretical successes followed and I was soon in line for a move to a new station as a Leading Firefighter.

My itchy feet had been signalling again and the lack of activity during the quiet times on watch had taken their toll. When not racing to calls, although kept busy with community safety activities, training and testing equipment, the thrill and distraction of the turnout was the only thing that allowed me to remain positive and for the most part, reasonably normal. When I say 'normal', I was very careful not to allow the lads to witness some of the less normal procedures that I needed to undertake. Perhaps it was an unnecessary inconvenience given that my reputation had little value, but all the same I did not want to provide further evidence that I was without doubt, the one piece of the jigsaw that didn't quite fit. It's horrible constantly feeling like the odd one out but I suspect that would have been my nature with or without the breakdown.

Checking breathing apparatus sets at the start of each shift was something that had always presented problems for me. The only piece of equipment capable of ensuring survival in life and death situations was always likely to create difficulties.

I attended an incident in the early months of my career and had entered an old farmhouse as part of a team of two, for search and rescue. The elderly lady sleeping on the ground floor was beyond saving due to the intensity of the fire and our task was to check the remainder of the property. We rushed into the extremely hot and smoke-filled hallway, found the staircase and headed for the bedrooms. My facemask was fitted with five securing straps (the spider), but felt loose and I began losing air by the bucket load. Finding the landing and attempting to search and maintain contact with my team leader, I was having to hold the mask to my face at the same time. Large, smoke-logged and, unlike most domestic properties previously encountered, my partner disappeared into one of many rooms and I lost him for a few minutes. The floor had been burned away in places due to the intensity of the fire below and, concerned that my air would be insufficient to complete the task, I wondered if my obvious lack of attention to detail during the earlier check was going to be my final defining moment.

It proved not to be, as my partner suddenly appeared out of the smoke and we continued together searching the last few rooms before exiting the building and giving the all clear to the gaffer. By now everyone knew that I had used too much air for the length of time I had been deployed and with great embarrassment I had to report the problem with my mask. Strangely enough, no comments were made and as time wore on I realised that my brush with disaster had been a timely reminder to all. The spider was often neglected during the daily check because it was always intact and there was no reason for it to be otherwise.

Someone on the previous night shift must have left it in that condition and I had missed it.

The event was a definite kick in the rear for me and unfortunately something that created some considerable angst at the start of each and every shift. I wonder if anyone ever noticed that the two minutes spent checking their set was considerably less than the five, ten, fifteen or so minutes that I needed to be satisfied mine was safe. Not for me you understand, because I was expendable. Had it been only for my benefit, two minutes would have been sufficient, but what if the next wearer failed to check properly?

I would often appear at the tea table only to hear the words, 'OK, boys, back to it.' I was never asked why I rarely made that trip up the single flight of stairs in time. They must have known, because I would be left in the rear of the truck long after everyone had departed. Even on the good days, after timely completion, the nervous tension and sweat was difficult to hide. Probably a good thing then, that promotion beckoned and the routines as a leader would allow for someone else to check my set for me. That would be a welcome relief.

Little did I know that the rules were different at different stations and my new boss would insist that we should each take responsibility for our own equipment. I couldn't argue with the directive as I could imagine the alternative: 'You checked his set, so it's your fault.'

Strange how I could do all the things required of me in critical situations but my brain wouldn't allow peace of mind in the most innocuous of circumstances. Needless to say my meticulous standards remained for as long as I rode the big red trucks and one thing I can say for sure is that no one would ever find a defect with a set that I had tested or serviced. Many hours may have been wasted over the years but nobody could accuse me of complacency or lack of attention to matters of safety.

31. The shooter.

That statement reminds me of an occasion many years ago when I *had* been complacent and downright careless. Probably the first time I had been a real danger to my family. I was ten years old and as Dad was fond of guns and all things free, poaching being one of his favourite pastimes, he thought it would be fun to show me the ropes. Some family friends lived in the shadow of the Wrekin hill, a well-known Shropshire landmark and a few thousand years ago, an active volcano. These friends owned a number of assorted firearms and had the use of acres of land upon which to hone their marksmanship. Mum wasn't too sure about the idea but her influence was pretty much zero and so the target practice commenced soon after our arrival. My sisters were all happily exploring the house and surrounding countryside with the eleven-year-old twins looking after the little ones, aged seven and four.

I was so excited at being allowed to fire a real pellet gun at small targets fixed to a post in the garden and with the blessing of the adults I persevered for about half an hour until one shot flew extremely wide of the mark and whistled its way through the hedge bordering the adjacent field. Seconds later I heard the giggling voices of my sisters who had been walking in the field on the other side of the hedge. Frozen where I stood, I looked around for some kind of support. No adults in sight and my heart beating fit to burst through my chest, I dropped the rifle and raced to the boundary. Far too short to see over the foliage I squinted through a gap at about waist height.

There they were, all four happily continuing on their way, running toward the woods at the foot of the extinct volcano. My heart continued to pound as I wondered if I should tell, if I should own up that I nearly killed one of my sisters. Of course I would go directly to the house and confess. They would understand that it had been an accident and see that no harm had come as a result of my stupidity. I walked across the neatly tended lawn and tried to remember the timing of the incident. Had the giggles reached my ears before the shot had been fired or after? Doubts had been raised in my fragile, impressionable mind and for months I forensically analysed those few minutes to make sure I had got the facts straight. I think I was innocent and had tortured myself just because I was made that way.

The adults merely told me to be more careful next time. They didn't seem to understand how close they had been to losing a child.

Still troubled by the overpowering sense of guilt, I was later marched into the field with a shotgun over my shoulder. It was a twelve-bore and Dad had been keen to impress on me that it had a kick like an angry donkey. The recoil would be enough to throw me backwards and probably bruise my shoulder into the bargain.

I am not sure what time of year it was but there was an abundance of rabbits and Dad wanted me to get my first kill. To make things easier for me, whilst reminding me that I didn't have the strength to handle a real gun, he passed me a smaller bore weapon, I think it was called a

4/10. This would be a piece of cake, I thought, and feeling comfortable with the weight, I lifted it to my shoulder and squinted through the sights in the general direction of a furry brown creature. I couldn't do it, I couldn't pull the trigger. Realising that Dad would not appreciate this blatant lack of courage I aimed above its ears and into the woods and as the barrel jerked sharply into the air I watched a little white tail bobbing out of sight. I was overjoyed but I was frightened to show it. Does that make me a good person? I like to think so.

32. Oh brother!

The old man lay motionless in the hospice bed, his skin hanging from his bones and his face looking more skeletal by the day. The cancer that had been eating his body for the last few years had finally succeeded in breaking his spirit and taking away any dignity he had managed to salvage from a life of self-destruction. Uncle Jack made a sucking sound with his lips as I gently placed the small pink sponge stick against them. Watching over him as there was no close family to accompany him in his final hours, I was told I could use it to moisten his lips with water.

Stubborn to the end he dragged the water from the sponge and swallowed awkwardly. He was so close to death that I failed to heed the instructions and contrary to my normal reaction I felt no guilt despite imagining that my actions may have been speeding up his journey to meet my old man in heaven or in hell. Fleeting thoughts of how it must have been my intention to kill him were almost insignificant as I sensed his need to drink and couldn't bring myself to refuse him his last wish. He was unable to speak or open his eyes but I could sense the pleasure it gave him. I watched him slip away, silently.

I didn't despair, torture myself or seek reassurance on this occasion because for once my heart and head were on the same side and after confessing to the nurse that he had taken in some fluid, she smiled with sympathy, touched my arm and walked away.

He was Dad's slightly younger brother and had taken the wrong path in life, spending most of his life in prison. The very first time I saw him was in the early '70s when he pulled up in his car outside the house and spoke to Dad briefly before driving away. What I recall as a few months later but was more likely at least a year, I noticed a report in one of the daily newspapers, the *Daily Mirror* I think, that an armed robbery in Liverpool had resulted in the shooting of a security guard. The guard was a husband and father and would later die of gunshot wounds. My uncle and two other men were jailed for life and I subsequently discovered that the unexpected visit to our home was to encourage my gun-loving father to join him on the heist. Dad was a bit of a rogue but not a criminal and although he liked a few free rabbits and pheasants he drew the line at armed robbery. His death wish for farmers had clearly been a macho boast that was in some strange but sincere way designed to make me feel better.

To this day I am not sure who actually pulled the trigger on that fateful day, but suffice to say that Uncle Jack spent over twenty five years in prison, finally being released on licence in the late '90s. He had no family but Mum, having known him as a young lad when she first met Dad, felt the need to help him to adjust to the outside world and he eventually settled in the town a few miles away from my home. I got to know him and struggled to understand how such a gentle, kind and quiet man could have been involved in such a terrible crime. He only had a few years on the outside because the lung cancer that had taken away part of his lung whilst inside, came back with a vengeance and with Mum away and unable to tend to him, I witnessed the end in her place.

He would have seen this undignified demise as getting his just desserts, but for me watching a man whom I had only known as a kindly uncle, disappear in front of my eyes was a very humbling experience. He was already gone but that tiny sip of water made me feel better and for once my rational brain told me that this little intervention, despite being against the rules, was a sign of my sensitive, caring nature rather than that of some sinister human being.

33. The builder. My friend.

The builder had supported me to a level I found almost inconceivable and had assisted me through some difficult times without even knowing his contribution. He had made it possible for me to remain occupied for the majority of my waking hours, meaning that although new and equally terrifying obsessions were introduced depending on the circumstances, I at least gained some respite from the fears of causing harm to my family. Sitting astride the ridge of a dilapidated roof in all weathers and working away with little or no concern for my own safety was just the tonic my brain needed to drive away the pain and anxiety that was by now just part of me.

Ladders at ridiculously steep or shallow pitch, cutting slates in the rain with the electric angle grinder, all were fraught with personal risk and I should have known better but it did not matter. This manner of replacement therapy featured heavily in the coming years and along with physical exertion, it has been my greatest ally, providing me with a greater resilience and additional strength to continue the fight. Medication has had a minimal stabilising effect, just taking the edge off, allowing me to avoid pressing the panic button, but no more than that.

The builder was oblivious to my evil intent and it doesn't bear thinking about, how often he had a lucky escape. The hammer, the screwdriver, the pencil, everything was a weapon in my hands. The hours I spent battling the inner me, the confusion, the pressure of proving my innocence, trying to focus on the job in hand whilst contemplating a horrific alternative that he could never have imagined. Some were just fleeting thoughts that many people must experience, so why did I expand and elaborate to a point where my mind almost accepted the inevitable? A sudden, frenzied, and merciless attack!

He walked in on me on several occasions whilst I gazed at the wall, unable to apply the mortar because I needed to establish some kind of rule in my head, counting to ten and repeating until it felt right. He would ask me what was wrong and I would just smile and say that I was revising some technical details in preparation for my station manager's exam. He would walk away and I felt vulnerable because he had caught me out. He must have known I was troubled again after the first episode, but he said little other than offering me a cup of his milky coffee, a sandwich, a chocolate bar. Sometimes I didn't know if he actually liked me or simply valued my work. The wages had increased since the early days so I decided that it must be down to affection.

There is a positive side to all the negativity and difficulty I faced whilst hiding from my family. It makes it sound like he was my very own guinea pig, someone to practise on in an attempt to silence the thoughts. Perhaps he was exactly that, because his presence provided some of the exhilarating highs that came from proving to myself that I had no harmful intentions. It could stimulate a euphoric reaction where the thrill of controlling the curse was the ultimate reward. I liken it to being high on drugs, sexual conquests, the thrill of a good deed completed, goals scored or being the man who comes top in the interview process. The euphoria rarely lasted more than a few minutes before being replaced by the next and equally demanding challenge.

Once in a while it could last for a couple of days but only if I was extremely lucky and it happened to strike during a peak in my mood rather than in the midst of one of those all-too-regular troughs. I was only as good as my last fight, and if that was a loss, the task of proving myself would always lead me closer to the edge. I needed to up the ante, increase the risk of harming him to allow me to emerge free from guilt. My mind would finally allow me to turn away in disgust, discard the thoughts and bury myself in the depths of despair.

Turning away was always the hardest part because I knew the doubts would return and erase the evidence, but at least when I returned home, the sickness was confined to the trauma of the day and nothing to do with my children. My thoughts would still turn to those focused on ending my life but one look at the little smiling faces gave me the strength to try one more day. The next day with the builder could be one with little or no fear and all would be well, or equally as likely the wrong move; the accidental brush of the shoulder, the inadvertently placed trip hazard could wreak havoc.

One day, the builder knelt on the floor to do something, I can't quite remember what. His position immediately influenced my thought processes, but feeling strong and not needing to hover, not repeating or ritualising as I stood over him I walked away, confident and determined. I returned to continue my task, whatever that was at the time, and the mood changed. I don't know why, I could never explain, but the desire to reassure myself was sudden and relentless. No tools, no risks, apart from my bare hands. A new concept.

He gave a shout as he moved to a different position. The wire brush had shed some of its needles and one had pierced his lower leg, puncturing a varicose vein. Blood loss from these damaged veins can be significant and has proved fatal in some cases. Those thought processes formerly threatening mutiny, immediately switched to care and his well-being and the flow of blood, often extremely difficult to stem, was my new objective.

I sat him on the bottom stair, raised his leg above the level of his heart with some old milk crates and wrapped the wound tightly with the cleanest rag I could find. He was lucky as the puncture was below a blockage in the knotted vein and after taking him home and getting an all clear from the surgery, I was a Samaritan, an all-round good guy. But what about the blood? The attempts at washing were pointless; we all know how difficult it is to get rid of DNA evidence. I would need a concerted effort to avoid contaminating the children and had to go straight to the bathroom and leave the cuddles until later.

The eternal question remains in my head: if eventually I come to the conclusion that all is well, why not think as the crow flies and save the time, the effort and pain? The simple answer is that although sometimes I can do just that, I have to be sure that neglecting the process of proving my innocence does not set in motion fresh, and more troubling rituals. Ignorance of the law, my law, is no excuse.

34. The ferry.

Five children, ranging in age from thirteen to thirty and never have any of them been in danger but during those three decades, each has been the focus of intrusive thoughts at one time or another. This is the hardest thing in the world to share but my love for them has never been in doubt, and knowing that they all understand me and have no fear or desire to run away, allows me a little peace of mind.

Daily activities with the children always had a huge impact on me with the threat of danger lying around every corner and the possibility that innocuous events could result in catastrophe ever in my mind. The more the brain dwells on compulsive and impulsive thoughts, particularly if those thoughts are of a potentially damaging nature, the more likely that the chemically deficient OCD brain will establish its own rules, its own direction and its own creative outcomes.

The ferry was packed and the journey from Dover to Calais was a new experience for us all. One adult member of the party was petrified of boat travel, in fact scared of most means of transport apart from those limited to four wheels and tarmac. The need to keep the costs of the trip to Spain to a minimum necessitated cheap travel which in turn required twenty four hours of driving and a channel crossing.

The anxiety exuded by the nervous traveller soon transferred to me and although my fears had always related to protection of the children, my brain was quick to react in the familiar frightening way. The fear of, and particularly the depth of, the cold, choppy water had already influenced a change in my thought processes, making me wonder if the survival rate at this time of year was as small as I imagined. Man overboard was something I was bound to consider given my chaotic mind and its affinity for danger.

The children, as children do, wanted to feel the excitement of the journey, and despite my absolute horror at the suggestion I summoned the strength to escort them on to the deck so that we could all (apart from the nervous traveller) experience the fresh sea air, the cool breeze and the heaving of the ferry as it rose and fell whilst ploughing through the grey blue swell.

The youngest of the children was too small to see over the rails that surrounded the viewing deck and was often carried for convenience. He was begging to be picked up. I knew that this was a bad idea and my stomach churned as I pondered some terrifying scenarios. What if I stumbled and dropped that little bundle over the rails into the cold, churning waves? What if I was pushed by one of the other passengers and we both tumbled overboard? The sickness I felt was all too familiar and the thoughts became more horrific by the second.

The children all grinned at me, their gleeful faces met by my forced smile. My OCD brain was planting the seed of despair. My arms also felt that overwhelming sickness, a sensation that I likened to a fear of heights. I could relate to that feeling, being the experienced firefighter, always required to deal with such situations with a steely resolve. I imagined that this sense of paralysis in my upper body was something one would feel if frozen with fear from some form of unexpected marauding attack. My whole body was reacting to the fear I had cultivated and I started to wonder if this was actually a disguise, a fake, because I wasn't really concerned about the danger, I was actually feeling a real and tangible 'urge' to launch my son into the air.

My heart missed several beats and I backed away from the rails. The power of my mind made me feel like a murderer, a monster; it made me realise just how evil I must be. How could I prove that the thoughts were only thoughts? By this time in my life I had failed to reach any conclusion about OCD and expected it to haunt me forever. Could I maintain the façade of innocence and convince everyone around me that I was normal? Once again I foolishly decided to test myself and then it would be obvious that I would never harm anyone. Despite being fully aware of the naivety of the decision, my desperate need for reassurance just begged for more of the same as I sought stronger evidence of my pure intentions.

I returned to the rails and told myself to throw the child over the side. *Blank your mind off and just do it if you want to.* Not doing it would obviously prove my innocence. So I stood looking down at the heaving ocean with that awful thought in my head. I paused for just a few moments, feeling disgusted with myself before dragging all three of my offspring to the lower deck. My mind told me that this time I nearly did it.

I sat in a dejected and depressed state until we reached Calais. I had failed in my feeble attempt to beat the curse but I had clearly established that I had no right to call myself a father. Crying on the inside I tried to focus on the next part of the journey, knowing that I would face further challenges along the way and that this episode would remain in my mental computer until the return trip. Perhaps then I could prove that I didn't want to do it. I would have the perfect opportunity to redeem myself.

35. Turn to God.

Desperate times require desperate measures and perhaps there existed some kind of spiritual answer. Maybe that is why I had failed to see the light and continued to walk in the wilderness. My GP suggested that I join her congregation because for her it meant salvation. I remembered the rituals all those years ago protecting Mum night after night, and toyed with the idea that perhaps my ramblings were real prayers and I had always been destined to take a journey into righteousness.

My daughter wanted to come with me and so, with great enthusiasm and not sure what to expect, we entered the second floor meeting room to see a Born Again Christian gathering about to get under way.

The room was packed with people of all ages, lonely people, happy people, troubled people and all of them no doubt suitably pious. I was, however, more than pleased that so many from all walks of life, all with important stories to tell, believed they would have their questions answered by an unseen but ubiquitous God. The perfect solution, the meaning of life, joy and family values all neatly packaged on a Sunday morning. The hand waving and chanting, praising, bowing and swaying were all testament to their loyalty. Not for me, I realised immediately, though my daughter found it hugely entertaining, humming to the cheerful tunes, watching the 'funny ladies' hug and dance. I appreciated the opportunity to test the water but was convinced of my future abstinence when the church leader approached me at the behest of my doctor friend.

'Welcome, Oliver, is there anything you would like to ask me?'

Feeling slightly unnerved I raised the only logical question I could bring to mind at the time. I asked him why, if God was the answer for so many people, why was it that He had chosen to take my dad away at such a young age? Why was it that my sister had to see the pain etched upon Dad's distorted face and his lifeless body when his heart had exploded with one momentous final beat? Surely all the bad in the world would not exist if God had His way.

'People cause pain, Oliver, it's done for a reason, and there are reasons for everything.' The answer was not good enough for me.

I thanked him for his time and escorted my little girl to the landing feeling concerned and finding it impossible to accept that my dad had encouraged his own early demise because of his poor diet, sedentary lifestyle and lack of awareness. I am sure that is what this stranger had meant and I didn't want to hear that; I wanted to hear something positive, something that would create some belief in an all-powerful being. Moving down the first flight of stairs carrying my little girl, I caught sight of the ground floor entrance and it was like I was on the ferry once more, except the sea was a cold, hard surface. I knew then that God would not be my saviour. I moved away from the bannister and brushed against the wall as I descended because I couldn't bear to look at the sea below.

*

What about hypnotherapy? That had to be a solution, if only I could get to the bottom of it all. Maybe I could teach myself to meditate, to switch off completely and emerge with a sense of enlightenment and peace. The sessions were incredibly expensive but they had to be worth it. Reclining in the huge leather chair, gentle, soft music and the therapist's smooth, reassuring voice all added to the tranquillity. He told me I would feel sleepy, relaxed and empty of all thoughts. I should concentrate on something pleasant and allow myself to drift away. I was so determined to make it work, I was desperate to wipe the slate clean and start afresh without a care in the world.

After many sessions and very much poorer, I finally realised that I just wasn't the type to go under. Perhaps I was too tense, my mind unwilling to let go, distractions popping into my brain uninvited and sabotaging the process. Perhaps my doubts about hypnosis refused to let me believe; perhaps my doubts were reality.

Relaxation techniques, now that may not have solved all aspects of my condition but it may point the way to a better life. I tried and failed. I am sure it was my fault because I couldn't let go. My need to control the environment to prevent danger was compromised, I needed to be vigilant and ready for anything. The slightest slip, the smallest mistake could result in tragedy and I would be to blame. Better to remain alert and suffer the consequences than try to ignore the danger signs. Something would come along one day that would put everything into perspective and allow me to lead a normal life.

It must be a good day today because I am feeling positive and know that I can handle life. I tell myself that apart from fate, only I can change things, only I can manage the direction of my mind. I already know that I have a creature in there somewhere, creating havoc and it's about time I did some serious zoo keeping before the creature destroys me.

36. The beginning of the end.

Years passed with lightning speed, the birth of my third child making my first family complete. The timing of each pregnancy was entirely down to fate as my ex-wife forgot to take her contraceptive pill on each occasion at three yearly intervals and also forgot to tell me until the deed was done.

Having said that, with the marriage on the rocks from the minute we tied the knot, my three beautiful, adult children remain one of the few things that keep me reasonably sane and for the most part keen to stay alive during the darkest times.

Sometimes we fail to notice that life is passing us by and we forget to live in the now, concentrating on the past and understandably hoping for a better future. There came a point when enough is enough, however, and I began to sense a sea change in my domestic circumstances. Long had my sexual exploits been hidden from view but things started to unravel, indiscretions out in the open, it was make or break time.

My relationships with the fairer sex had remained a powerful influence on my ability to survive. I could use the thrill of the chase, the capture and the horizontal activity to ease my aching brain. I obsessed about the number of times I could rise to the occasion, how long I could delay the final thrust, how much pleasure I could provide. The success of each liaison was measured in quantity and quality and being asked to do it all over again was all the encouragement I needed to imagine my macho status. What red-blooded male wouldn't want to be a sexual athlete, a valuable commodity amongst the female fraternity? Delusional maybe, but it served a purpose at the time. Marriage was irrelevant because whilst I was playing the field, I had less time to worry about family life. Yes, the guilt could strike at any time, but it was never enough to prevent the wandering. I am not trying to justify infidelity but that is the way it was, and confident that I wasn't the only one with guilty secrets, I didn't see it as a problem.

Not until I met my second wife over twenty years ago did I start to realise the importance of stability in a relationship. My history with women was a disaster area and suffice to say at the age of thirty three, I finally grew up. The desire for one conquest after another, adding notches to my bed post, became an unnecessary burden because aside from my newfound contentment, each carefully concealed notch would, by the power of obsessional thought, be removed ready to be replaced by the next sexual encounter. Believe it or not, the power of my brain could convince me that nothing had taken place, but it wasn't as a means of protecting me from the guilt of transgression, it was my brain's way of telling me I hadn't succeeded in my quest to achieve manliness. I could have a one-night stand and within hours feel convinced that it didn't happen. The strategy had been far less traumatic than some alternatives would ever be and as a temporary measure it certainly hit the spot.

With the family now requiring more room to flourish it was time to extend our modern semi-detached house. I commenced work on a huge extension, increasing the number of bedrooms to five. Why five? I have no idea but someone must have considered it a necessity. The relationship grew more tiresome and whilst continuing to fill every waking hour with work and illicit play I was advised of a requirement to attend a nine-week course at the Fire Service college in the Cotswolds. Holding everything together was proving difficult but with a momentous shove and no shortage of obsessional drive I managed to complete the extension before leaving, thus removing a considerable burden. It wasn't enough to satisfy my endless desire for self-ruin though, and I found myself confessing to a recent period of infidelity.

The first five weeks of the course were based on operational competence and proved to be a challenging yet enjoyable break from all that had passed in recent years. No time for rituals or intrusive thoughts, other than the usual focus on being the best I could. During the first week at the end of one of my daily phone calls to speak to the children, my wife advised that the new year would bring fresh challenges in the shape of divorce, finding somewhere to live, and facing the fact that I was about to lose everything. I spent a few weekends travelling with newfound friends to their homes rather than going home and Christmas came with an agreement that I could sleep on the sofa just so that I could be with the children on that special day.

Having had no physical contact with my wife for many months I found it strange that she pounced on me unexpectedly one evening when all was quiet upstairs. In accordance with tradition and not being one to disappoint, the sympathy sex proceeded with little pomp or ceremony. With no further thoughts of getting back together or making any attempt to reconcile our differences the mould was cast and she filed for divorce whilst I was away finishing the second part of the course.

The large house, the new extension and the daily contact with the children had gone. The finality of it all hit me hard and I wasn't sure if it was going to be the start of the rest of my life or the beginning of the end of my life.

37. Divorce is a dream.

Divorce is sometimes considered to be one of the most likely causes of stress-related illness in modern life. Whilst this may be the case for many, for me it was almost a relief from the tried and tested anxiety formula that I had perfected. What wouldn't be? The initial period of solitude and weekly separation from my offspring was extremely difficult and I don't think I would be human if I had been immune from that. However, apart from the early months, when I needed to adjust to my life in the little terrace a stone's throw from the family home, the experience brought a certain amount of positivity and promise for the future.

Weekends with my children were full of all the things I had previously found so difficult. Trips to the park, swimming, games on the green outside the house and takeaway food under a blanket in front of the television. My obsessions were confined to the old favourites: the cleaning, personal hygiene and household safety routines, security, and convincing myself that accidental bumps and bruises were purely that. The more extreme issues were firmly confined to the back burner. I was just too busy and too happy, enjoying the company of a demanding toddler, an energetic, football-mad six-year-old and an emerging princess who at the tender age of nine was showing signs that perhaps she was more than a chip off the old block.

The occasional slide into harmful territory was usually confined to a Sunday evening when it was time for home and I would wearily, and with no shortage of dread, consider the empty week ahead. The need to make the weekends fun and to maintain a relaxed approach to fatherhood for the first time in many years was hard but so rewarding. I had to ensure that they wanted to come again the following week and was always petrified that a better offer would come along and persuade them otherwise.

My shifts, at the time consisting of two days followed by two nights, rolling forward each week by a day meant that the scheduling was difficult and for that reason I often had to negotiate, deceive and lie in order to guarantee a reasonable level of polite communication with my ex. New relationships in plain sight were impossible as the children became valuable currency. The first sign of any dalliance was punished with the threat of a weekend alone. Some days they would arrive only to be tempted by an unexpected visit from their mother who, with an innocent slip of the tongue, would mention a fun outing that was impossible to refuse, especially for the youngest. Mind games and manipulation became a regular theme.

The bombshell that she was pregnant again with a Christmas present baby was the last thing I needed. I soon found that the monotony and misery of lonely weeks without the children gave me plenty of time to speculate about the rewards of a poorly timed mid-divorce romp. The days often dragged, long and depressing, willing on the time when I could once again play Dad. Keeping busy and physically challenged was the most important strategy I had learned over the years, but finding it increasingly more difficult to fill the empty space with meaningful activities I became fixated on the only issue I had no control over. This baby, was it mine, what would I do, how should I react, why would anyone allow such a lack of judgment under the circumstances? I initially put these concerns down to my natural instinct for beating myself up.

Later, I discovered that my nine-week training course had prompted some less than scrupulous activity on the part of my ex, leading me to understand the true origins of the festive season fertilised egg. Strange coincidences, her rumoured romantic liaisons and increased familiarity with my nomadic younger cousin soon prompted a realisation that I needed to distance myself from the new child, much to the disgust of his older siblings who were blinkered into believing that Dad was being cruel to his baby.

I spent many months wrestling with my lack of love and concern for the child that it became an obsession in itself, eating me away and almost convincing me that I should ignore my indisputable knowledge and give the child a family. My self-doubt and her convincing plea for reconciliation and sworn truth of paternity, prevented me from moving on for almost a year. The children were ever more determined to reunite the family and my absolute fear of losing them almost tipped the balance and I finally decided to tell them what I knew. Their mum said I was mental, deluded and evil and for many years I am certain that I was universally considered to be entirely lacking in moral fibre and humility.

To make matters worse, my theory that the new job would provide some respite from the previous onslaught of character assassination was entirely unfounded. My reputation was so well travelled that it was as the old idiom says, 'like going from the frying pan into the fire'.

Functioning on pure willpower and very little else I found myself taking more time off work to recharge my batteries in a bid to return wearing my usual mask of normality. The problem was that I wasn't normal; the pressure the pretence created during working hours felt like I was having to hold my breath underwater for too long. Finally, when the last pocket of air had been released from my lungs and the impulse to breathe was too great, the water entered. Temporarily slowed by the automatic response protecting the airway I would run for home and shut myself away from the world until I needed to pull myself together, ready to welcome the children once more.

Even though I harbour little or no bitterness towards my work colleagues, I have to admit that the bigotry and ignorance and lack of respect for unseen illness was remarkable. The seemingly common perception was that mental illness was something to be at worst, mocked and ridiculed, and at best, hidden from society, an embarrassment for friends and family. But what could I do, how could I expect to change that perception when I felt embarrassed, ashamed, and humiliated myself by my apparent inability to live like a normal human being?

They hadn't experienced such behaviour within their Fire Service and therefore couldn't be expected to consider it an illness just like any other. Consider me on the other hand, suffering for so many years, struggling and fighting, with small victories here and there, surely I knew all there was to know about OCD. More than twenty years had passed and I was still around and to the casual observer, behaving much like anyone else, aside from perhaps a few noticeable quirks. But we all have those, don't we?

Yet even I couldn't agree that this was a normal illness, this was not like any other physical ailment, because it was weird and unpredictable. It could never be likened to proper, sensible, sad illnesses, where sympathy was well deserved. My childish wish to exchange all that I knew for a tangible, more physical affliction never diminished because I was so scared that I would be permanently labelled the 'strange one' and saddled with the stigma and disgrace of spending time in an asylum.

38. Strange one, or just the odd one out.

Competent and capable, on the surface I was always well treated and respected as a junior officer. I managed to portray the professional face of the service at all times, betraying what was really happening on the inside. Perhaps it was my perception and partly influenced by paranoia, but I could not quite allow myself to relax completely because I was constantly looking for the wary eye, anticipating suspicion and the tentative manner in which certain factions tended to engage with me. I initially assumed that the smiling face whose mouth uttered the words, 'Hello strange one' was signalling friendship and acceptance. It was not too long before I realised that the knowing glances, innuendo and inconsistent behaviour meant something quite different. I decided to pretend that it was all to do with comedy value or a simple lack of sensitivity, accepting that there was no real malice intended. I turned the other cheek and replied with similar sarcasm, just hoping that I was not becoming something of a sideshow, a target for institutional ignorance.

Difficult days spent alone at home were normally followed by quiet nights at work offering much of the same. Times were changing within the service and where once we grouped together during stand-down time, playing darts, cards and snooker or gathering to watch the latest movie or video, there was now a tendency for the group to fragment; twos and threes in various corners of the station passing the time until midnight signalled the time when sleep was allowed.

I was comfortable with any company and to a certain extent the feeling was reciprocated but because of the underlying doubts, remaining a slave to the illness and general weariness with life I regularly slipped away to my sleeping bag earlier than many of my colleagues. Being a Leading Hand I really ought to have tried harder to be a better role model but I was never the first in bed and I could always pretend I was reading a good book or doing some private study.

Sleep always eluded me despite my medication having a greater effect later in the evenings when it would encourage weariness and lethargy. Not settling in the main dorm because of the sound of wart hogs destroying the tranquillity with their loud snoring, I tucked myself away in a secluded corridor and spent many hours alone, sometimes racked with anxiety and contemplating the uninvited thoughts from earlier in the day. Tears would occasionally distract me from the anticipation of the next shout and I tried hard to remember that I was there to do a job and could soon be required to spring into action, leaving the baggage behind.

Finally, due to mental exhaustion I would slip into a deep sleep and succumb to the repetitive nightmares that had by now become so familiar. I was in a prison cell. I didn't know why I was there but had obviously committed some awful crime and I would see someone who looked like me tearing at the walls, protesting innocence and begging for leniency. Perhaps it was the asylum and I was finally receiving the images from dreams that had previously eluded me, the dreams that had delivered my insight into a Victorian era. I would wake in a cold sweat and after taking a while to confirm my surroundings I would realise I was a free man. My fear of cracking completely and carrying out some horrendous crime was a constant reminder that in emotional terms I would always be a prisoner.

39. Vulnerable children.

It was around this time that I took a turn for the worse and couldn't look at a lone child in the street without feeling angry and concerned that they were unsupervised. This day and age with all the bad in the world, murderers and abusers, vicious thugs and sexual predators, and not an adult to be seen. Neither could I look at a vulnerable person or a homeless man without feeling sorry for his plight, sympathetic that the world had somehow let him down in his hour of need.

This would never just remain a feeling of sadness and desire to make everything better, as I would begin to worry that my feelings of concern were not an indication of my true intentions. The intrusive thoughts were not going away in a hurry. There was no escape from them; they appeared from nowhere for no apparent reason other than for the sole purpose of destroying me.

Ashamed to admit it, but at the same time relieved that the danger to my own children had apparently eased I experimented with the tablets, trying to find a miracle before it was too late. Fleeting moments of calm during the little peaks of happiness when I knew that it was all in my mind gave me some fresh hope. The weekly fix provided by the kids when I only needed to handle typical OCD rituals and compulsions were almost surreal, as I lived like any other parent. Covert liaisons with the opposite sex were increasingly possible as the ex was in a relationship and therefore less interested in me and this helped to ease the pain, but the end of family time always signalled the start of another tough period. If only I could switch this thing off.

At the start of a shift one evening in late autumn a report of a fire in the woods was met with the usual moan of disappointment, crews generally yearning for the more exciting and challenging jobs. It was school holiday time and we had received several similar calls to this particular area as a result of bored youngsters attempting to make their half-term break more exciting. Setting small rubbish fires on the local recreation area and in the woodland adjacent to the community centre was becoming the trend and consequently a regular frustration for us.

With darkness already upon us, I was riding in charge of the pump and booked in attendance at the address. With no sign of fire in the locality, we commenced a search of the immediate area, initially concentrating on the surrounds of the community centre and the open ground. Minutes later a small group of youngsters approached us, all shouting at the same time, yelling instructions about where we would find the fire that the naughty lads had started. They all looked about five or six years old, but given the nature of the area and the level of social deprivation they could easily have been younger. It was never a surprise to witness toddlers wearing little more than a filthy disposable nappy, a dummy stuffed in their grimy little face, engaging with us on the estate whilst parents were elsewhere, oblivious to the whereabouts of their precious babies.

My longstanding dismay at how some parents allowed their youngsters to roam the neighbourhood unsupervised had already activated and I could sense a nervous anticipation in the pit of my stomach. Newspapers were always headlining stories describing terrible tragedies and horrific crimes in relation to small children and in accordance with my ability to assume the mantle of such perpetrators I dreaded the scenario that appeared to be unfolding.

Determined to remain in a group situation and not find myself isolated with the small people, I listened intently and followed one of my colleagues and the more persuasive youngster to the edge of the woods. She pointed into the darkness in the direction of a small gap in the trees and explained that she and her friends had seen the fire and 'stamped on it to put it out'. The evidence of her actions was plain to see on her shoes so I told her to go back to her friends and that we would take a look to make sure that it hadn't started again, not being particularly tactful in my attempt to send her on her way. She refused to budge, and against my better judgment the three of us moved towards the designated spot.

With tension building I was leading the small party when we entered a clearing where a smouldering collection of fabric, paper, twigs and cardboard struggled to find enough heat to remain alight. Empty beer cans, drug paraphernalia and other waste materials littered the ground, consistent with the teenage gang culture prevalent in this locality. Increasingly frustrated, I wondered again how it could be that these tiny humans were permitted to explore with complete freedom, oblivious to the danger they could face from people like me.

I radioed through to the pump operator asking for a couple of buckets of water. Waiting nervously, my thoughts took over and I descended into a place where my initial concern and annoyance was twisted into a fear of familiar harmful intent. I almost announced my heightened distress out loud and moved closer to my colleague and away from the child. I knew I didn't wish her any harm but I needed to prove it.

The opportunity arose sooner than I had expected as a shout from behind alerted us to a second seat of fire. My colleague ran in the direction of the call. I was stranded alone with a vulnerable little girl and I hated the isolation with an intensity unlike any other in the past. If someone had told me that I could feel so ill, without actually being ill, I would have ridiculed the notion. I crouched close to the smouldering pile as if investigating its origins and held my arms tightly by my sides. With trembling hands I gripped the underside of my thighs in an attempt to refuse my mind the opportunity to accuse me of laying a hand on my new assistant.

Whilst I pretended I was contemplating what to do next, the little girl chatted away incessantly and despite listening to her words I didn't hear what she was saying. I looked at her dirty little face which was roughly level with mine and I smiled briefly, quickly looking away as my mind was interpreting the smile as an attempt to foster trust and an ultimate betrayal.

Once again my body was repulsed by my hidden agenda and the sweat in the heavy and cumbersome fire kit became so overwhelming that I needed to remove my tunic. I was soaked, and the little girl broke the intensity of the moment by giggling and saying, 'Have you been squirted by your friends?' I smiled again at the cuteness and innocence of the comment but held my almost foetal position, my protective shell.

The wait for the buckets of water was over. The probationer approached and I raised my dispirited body and switched to professional mode in an instant. I convinced myself and any witnesses that all was well with my world and after one final stomp of the sludgy mass, we trudged back to the open space, the place where she was safe. Why had she been there? It was dark, it was cold and her parents should have known better. You never knew who was prowling, waiting for the chance to pounce. That time she was lucky.

40. Same old story.

There was a trip to the doctor the very next day with similar desperation to that of the evening of my admission to hospital some years earlier. On this occasion I had no support or friendly reassurance as the builder was no longer part of my inner circle. The doctor knew nothing of my history other than the snippets gleaned by way of a brief scan through my records two minutes before my arrival. My one ally in the medical profession was long gone and no doubt dealing with her own troubles with the help of the omnipotent Samaritan up in the heavens.

The answer was an increase in medication or perhaps a change to a more modern formula. Anafranil[3], now a close ally with my internal organs, and the trade name for clomipramine, was an early treatment for obsessional depressive disorders. It was known as a tricyclic antidepressant, acting on the nerve cells in the brain. Neurotransmitters, namely serotonin and noradrenaline are the chemical messengers between the nerve cells that when released, are believed to lighten mood. However, they no longer affect mood when they become reabsorbed by the nerve cells.

---

[3] netdoctor.co.uk

Depression is understood to decrease the amount of released feel-good chemicals from the brain's nerve cells. The drug works by preventing the reabsorption of serotonin and noradrenaline, thus helping to prolong the mood lightening effect and relieving the symptoms of depression. The effect on obsessive and compulsive traits is less known but the positive action delivered by the two friendly chemicals is believed to have an impact.

Developed in the early 1960s it is now often superseded by more modern drugs known as SSRIs, selective serotonin reuptake inhibitors. These also affect the levels of serotonin within the brain but despite their wide use both in Europe and in the USA, there is very little hard evidence of how they improve mood. Despite many attempts to transfer to this modern variety of brain drug, I was never able to get over the gradual reduction of my original recipe in order to introduce something new. The transition was always too difficult due to the onset of side effects and the materialisation of fresh doubts and a physically crushing feeling in my head.

My concern was that something had been working and now it wasn't. Whatever the Anafranil had achieved in recent years, all I cared about was that it had occasionally eased the depressive tendencies, bringing at least some respite and the odd period of relative stability. The more I had learned about the drug and those benefitting from the impact it had on their quality of life, the more I looked at it as some kind of wonder drug.

I agreed with the new doctor's opinion that it wasn't the time for me to wean myself off one long term drug in a further attempt to experiment with a more modern version that as far as I could tell, claimed to perform the same function.

The decision to increase my dose to double the previous level was a daunting prospect, and I was concerned about how I would cope even before I collected the prescription. Increased drowsiness, nausea, sleeplessness, lack of concentration and severe headaches were just some of my previous reactions and I feared there was worse to come. I began to consider some of the more severe side effects that appeared on the Anafranil information sheet such as sexual problems, aggressive tendencies and major organ malfunction. With the increased medication in my system, the idea that the standard ten to fifteen years of clinical trials was enough didn't exactly fill me with confidence. Perhaps I was being medicated to an early demise rather than choosing my own time to go.

Signed off from work for a month, I was struggling with life in general, sometimes through boredom, more often through despair, but constantly weary from the medication and the relentlessly chaotic brain activity. Gradually coming to the conclusion that I had to fight harder and that the tablets were only part of the solution, I resolved to be positive and think of my children who had always been my main inspiration. This must have been a sign that I was experiencing one of my good times, although I knew it wouldn't last.

I wished I could have the word 'peaks' tattooed on the inside of my eyelids as a permanent reminder of a brighter tomorrow. It has taken me many years to realise that such moments are part of the natural sequence of events and the hope that another one will come along in due course, possibly at exactly the right moment, needs to remain a constant in my brain. It was one of the flimsiest of lifelines, but maybe my tomorrows would provide the answers I craved.

41. A bridge too far. The troubled teen.

Late one evening in December, whilst at work after a few days of high anxiety influenced by attempts to reduce the medication again, I was startled by the turnout speaker at around two in the morning: a report of a person threatening suicide on the railway line at the town station about half a mile down the road.

In attendance within a few minutes we made our way to the railway bridge that towered high above the river. All rail traffic had been suspended and four of us approached a police officer at the far end of the bridge. Whilst still leaning over the steel hand rail, he briefly explained that a young female had climbed the frost-covered lattice work before descending into the murky blackness below. He had been pursuing her across the tracks in an attempt to apprehend her for what was at the time the serious offence of trespassing on railway property. She had threatened to throw herself into the freezing waters some forty feet below as she clambered awkwardly out of sight.

Without pausing to carry out the procedural 'dynamic risk assessment' and upon seeing the gaffer arriving with the crew of our second pump I, too, disappeared into the darkness. I was conscious that survival time in the winter water would be extremely short should she fall from the structure, either by accident or choice. Descending with caution I called out into the night, my breath coming in short, noisy gasps as the cold air hit my lungs. I heard nothing and continued downwards towards the huge brick and steel parapets that held the bridge above the swirling current. Was that a voice I could hear? It sounded like it was distant but the noise of the water against the piers and the wind buffeting the framework made it difficult to be sure. I called again and this time I was certain.

Below me and to the right on the ledge of one of the parapets I could see a small figure close to the edge. Slowly I made my way down, trying to make verbal contact as I climbed. Her words came in short bursts, sounding like the old comedian who pretended his microphone was playing up, fragmented, intermittent and echoing against the steelwork making it impossible to make out what she was saying.

I got steadily closer, talking as I approached, and it soon became clear that she was warning me not to move any nearer, threatening that she would jump if I failed to comply with her wishes. Finally alighting on the parapet about twenty feet to her right, I asked if she was OK and apologetically told her that I needed to sit and rest a while. I tried to find some humour and explained that the clambering in pursuit was a real challenge for someone of my age and without my taking a breather she would probably need to rescue me. Not convinced that the attempt to lighten the mood had succeeded, I precariously wedged myself with my back to the brickwork where I had just enough space to sit without my legs dangling over the edge. She was doing the same but was unfortunately some distance out of reach.

I sat for a moment and made idle conversation which seemed to be having no effect, when without warning the roar of a high revving boat engine thundered above the sound of the swollen river. Not quite at flood level but very near, the current was extremely powerful and dark shadows of floating debris were just about visible twenty five feet below me. Down to my left I could make out a spotlight though the steel work. The rescue boat based at our station had been deployed and the boat handler, without authority from the command point, was gunning the vessel towards the bridge. The girl shouted aggressively, yelling at me that she would jump if anyone came closer.

I reiterated her threat loudly into my handheld radio, urging the boat crew to abort, but it was too late, they were already speeding past the parapets below. She stood and moved forwards and I moved towards her, expecting the inevitable. Ten feet away now, she paused at the edge and I spoke to her again urging her not to do it, nothing could be that bad, believe me I knew.

She looked in my direction at the same time as the boat manoeuvred quickly out of sight, the voice of the gaffer up on the railway line booming over the radio, ordering the boat crew to leave the area immediately. I told her they were gone and that no one else would approach without her permission. She was obviously in a distressed frame of mind and I was too far away to make a grab for her.

Nervous seconds passed and she appeared to settle a little, so I asked her if she was OK and offered her my tunic for protection from the cold and chilling wind. She declined but I persisted, saying that if she was going to do something foolish then I too would see what the water was like this time of year. I told her that if she did it, I would make sure that she wasn't alone. She asked what I meant and I called her bluff. 'We could do it together, I probably have more problems than you,' I advised, gloomily.

She sat back down and I took my fire tunic off, lying that I was a bit warm anyway and if she felt like trying it out, she could. Placing it perhaps four feet away from where she stood I saw her glance for a moment and then move towards it. I was tempted to reach out but thought better of it, and realising that I was winning her confidence decided to delay until I was within striking distance.

Talking of 'striking', at no point was my mind confused because protecting a young life was my only priority. Looking back now though, perhaps the opportunity to become a hero also had a small part to play. Not sure if that's just me trying to attack my integrity but needless to say I was focused and ready, intrusive thoughts a million miles away.

I withdrew a little and watched as she struggled with the heavy Bristol fire tunic fabric, dragging it around her small shoulders and settling back into her original position. I was freezing within minutes but it was worth it as I felt that some ground had been gained. Chatting over nothing in particular I asked if she would mind me sitting next to her as I couldn't hear her very well, adding that we could stay all night if necessary.

She eventually agreed and I shuffled slowly to her side observing a very young, pretty face under a mop of lank, greasy, unkempt hair. She looked pained and pale in the residual light of my torch which I made sure remained in a position unlikely to imitate a spotlight for the purpose of interrogation. I avoided directing it at her face but I managed to note her tender years, probably around seventeen or eighteen I thought. Either way, a woeful end to whatever troubles had driven her to this point, an unlikely liaison in the dead of night. Time passed quickly as we chatted like old friends, both of us unable to decide who was the least fortunate.

The radio crackled for an update as two hours had raced by and the crews above us had been waiting patiently for a progress report. I was being offered a warm drink and food for the young lady, which she immediately but politely refused. Sarah was happy to talk at length about her lack of family support and her reasons for ending up in this predicament, candidly citing some previous psychiatric issues and a few run ins with the law.

I shared similar confessions (not the law bit) and explained that we had a lot in common and I understood how she felt. She told me she was eighteen years old and I smiled at her, saying that I had reached the tender age of thirty six and after all the trials and tribulations of my earlier years had finally come to the conclusion that the future held something positive for all of us.

42. Saviour.

We talked for another hour or so and eventually I asked if could put my arm around her shoulders so that I too could benefit from some of the warmth provided by the tunic. It made sense to me as I would at least have some control in the event of any sudden movements. Not being aware of her general health and frame of mind I was concerned that the slightest wrong word, noise or a change of direction in the wind could result in unpredictable behaviour and I needed to make sure I had the best chance to stop her in her tracks.

She leaned into me and I placed my arm loosely around her back. I sensed her vulnerability and imagined how I would feel if it were my daughter in the same fix, alone and unable to tell anyone how she really felt. It made me appreciate my life and humbled me to the extent that I made a promise that I would stay with her during the next phase of the adventure if she agreed to let me help her back to safety. The police would need to speak with her of course but I would make sure that no one grabbed her or handcuffed her, treated her like a criminal.

She made me promise that I would go with her to the police station if that was possible so that she had a friendly face as company. I checked with the command point on the platform and it was confirmed that if we ended the standoff the police would approve the request. She was obviously frightened by the thought of returning to an inevitable fate and the earlier boldness had gone and she tensed and moved away from me slightly. Needing to gain absolute trust to insure against the possibility of her backtracking on the agreement, I told a lie that I later paid for through the guilt it prompted when the drama was over.

My car keys were in my trouser pocket beneath my protective leggings and I removed a key and placing it into her cold little hand said that if she had nowhere to go she could use my spare room until she found her feet. This could never happen of course but at the time it persuaded a troubled and likeable young lady to give up on her quest and return to the tracks with me. I radioed through that we were on our way and the police and fire crews moved away from the bridge, retreating to the station platform.

Slowly we made our way to a short extension ladder that had been placed over the rail and on to the parapet to assist our ascent and I followed her tiny frame closely, watching every step. Stepping on to the track, I heaved a huge sigh of relief and immediately thought of the imminent trip to the Assistant Divisional Officer's desk to explain why I had gone against policy in descending into a risk area without safety equipment.

I didn't particularly care as I escorted Sarah to the platform where the police waited with my colleagues. Another section of ladder already in place, she climbed up and into the hands of two female police officers. They held her arms lightly and assisted her towards the Station Manager's office some twenty metres away from the platform. I followed closely and with a nod from the gaffer entered the office to sit beside the girl with whom I had spent the last four hours, only now seeing her as the child she really was. My sympathy grew as I listened to the police officer explaining what was going to happen next. Sarah asked again if I could go to the police station with her. She now seemed surprised that her request was re-confirmed, and seeing the relief on her face I stifled a tear, realising that from that point onwards, she would be on her own, there would be nothing more I could do.

Sitting in the police station whilst she was interviewed in the next room, I spotted the key sitting next to the few possessions she had placed on the waiting room table. Picking it up and reattaching it to my key ring I wondered if Sarah would understand. She never returned to the room, and I never saw her again as she was soon sent to 'Grisly Risley', a notorious female remand centre in Warrington, reputed to be one of the toughest and most uncompromising penal establishments in the country.

I feared for her, discovering later that it wasn't the first time she had spent time at Her Majesty's pleasure, being previously convicted of similar trespass offences and other indiscretions. She had attempted, or at least threatened, suicide on a number of occasions and I wondered if there really was a happy future lying in wait for her. With no close family, no fixed abode and a chequered past, the world must have been a lonely and bewildering place.

Criminal activities and mental illness regularly go hand in hand, yet do we understand the benefits of treatment and rehabilitation versus institutionalisation and stagnation? A few wrong turns, a different roll of the dice and perhaps my life would have been one of crime and punishment.

Years locked away in my world, more often than not, too self-absorbed to appreciate the reality that others face, I now realise that the grass is rarely a better shade of green somewhere over the bridge. For me at the time, Sarah was the source of a valuable lesson. Saddened and humbled but moving on regardless, I was congratulated on my supposed heroic rescue of the troubled teenager. There were no recriminations from the establishment, merely an arm around the shoulder and the promise of formal recognition.

The Chief Fire Officer's commendation failed to stimulate a feeling of pride but it made me realise that I may be one of the luckier ones in society. Despite my unique troubles and periods of desperation, I had precious dependants and they would always be my obsession, but I was eternally grateful that they would also continue to be my saviours.

43. Turning Point.

Life continued in a similar fashion and after a few months I hit a fairly buoyant patch, meeting a new partner, making it less easy to dwell in obsession mode during our time together. You just can't let people know the real you, at least until things get serious. I guess for most people, creating the right impression is a serious part of courtship, and for me it was doubly so. No one in their right mind would want to get heavily involved with me: fact!

A year of good times flew by with only the occasional hint of the old possessive nature creeping in, taking the place of some of the extreme baggage that had weighed me down previously.

There was no deceit intended of course, because as soon as I knew things were developing between us I confessed to the key events of my complicated past, and of course some of the less damaging behaviours were fairly obvious even to the uninitiated. I was still pretty much hung up on the risk of fire from smoking, often side-tracked by cleanliness issues, or harmful substances creeping into the home on my return from work because of incident related contamination. I was visibly over-protective with my three children who spent most weekends with us, but the most noticeable compulsion was in relation to her.

For the most part I was enjoying a caring, sharing, and happy relationship, something of a new experience for me, with respect and consideration on both sides. Becoming overtly possessive and jealous was the direction my mind decided to take and, of course, for me this was nothing new. What I failed to realise at the time and only recently came to terms with is that my suspicious mind and self-defeating, relationship-damaging inquisitions were part of the phenomenon that is OCD. You hear about insanely jealous and violent partners that metaphorically and literally suffocate their partners with incessant quizzing and controlling tactics. She was able to sustain the pressure based on the fact that my infuriating nature was purely designed for, and successful in, hurting myself and no one else.

I am certain that my insecurity became almost intolerable at times, but with no fear of physical harm and an overall average of good times filled with excitement, love and laughter, we grew from strength to strength. Lucky for me after twenty years we are stronger than ever and as an added bonus my wife has taught me to trust and to believe that relationships can work and if you are really lucky, you don't have to always watch your back.

Living together and building a home from our virtually derelict cottage was an exciting time, and coping fairly well with the issues that continued to disrupt what should have been an easy life, I was able to move gratefully into a new era. Before long, however, I forgot to manage the little things that had always managed to slowly evolve into far greater worries and I soon found myself slipping into the trap of relaxing too much and not showing enough respect to the unpredictability and complexity of OCD.

This eternal cycle was not new to me of course but the extreme lows never ceased to surprise me and it seemed that the more positive I became, the more likely it was that something would go wrong. Something would appear out of the blue to obliterate my newfound confidence and strength, leading me to suspect that the fear of trying and failing is what sometimes makes us decide not to bother, instead opting for a world of pessimism and uncertainty. But at least with such a philosophy nothing can burst your bubble because it has already been deflated.

It makes me think of the child that has a new pair of roller skates for Christmas and for fear of getting them dirty or damaged, keeps them safely in the box. The sunny day or change of mind-set prompts the child to open the box only to find that the skates no longer fit. If I followed the same path would there eventually be a time when I lost the ability to fit anywhere in this world? I resolved to try and stay positive instead.

Still waking every morning in the doldrums and taking a while to find the motivation to begin each day positively, I spent much of my free time trying to ease my depression with energy-sapping training sessions. Running, cycling, swimming; anything that would fatigue my body and provide some form of stimulation.

I had learned many years before that exercise increases blood calcium which in turn increases the production of dopamine, a chemical that is produced naturally in the brain. Exercise also increases endorphins which can produce effects similar to a dopamine high. These wonder chemicals had always provided some respite for me and I knew that if I could just get the drive to get out there and put physical demands on my body, the rest would take care of itself. Clearly not quite that simple but without exception coming back through the door was by far a more pleasurable journey than going out.

Thinking about it for a moment, perhaps this is why the disturbing ECT treatment, the effects of which I witnessed during the dark times, is still practised in the 21st century. Apparently, it too has the benefit of increasing dopamine levels. I wonder if Doug is still around and more importantly if the treatment finally turned out to be his personal salvation.

Exercising every day seemed to be encouraging a stability that had long been forgotten and although not replacing any of the obsessional behaviour it eased life for my partner and helped me to put things into perspective. With great enthusiasm I entered running races and trained with a local rugby team and for a while everything was going well. I felt fitter and healthier than I had for many years and reaped the benefits provided by the increase in good chemicals. Persuaded by some friends, I decided to do a bungee jump for charity. This was actually something I had always fancied doing but hadn't quite found the courage to make it happen. When the day arrived, unfortunately it coincided with a massive decline in my mood.

To use an analogy, I compare moods with a passenger lift serving the floors in a high rise building. Sitting on the ground floor the lift represented the everyday melancholy, ascending to the top floor delivered the extreme highs, whilst all floors between were the variations influenced by the peaks and troughs. The lift could also move from melancholy to the basement and on the day of the bungee jump the lift fell swiftly, careering out of control past every floor not stopping at the basement but continuing into what I suspect may have been the earth's molten core.

Maybe it wasn't that bad, perhaps I had been naïve and just forgotten once again, but I soon found myself in a different lift, suspended from a crane, being hoisted into position sixty five metres above the local garden centre. Just one of my children and a good friend in the crowd below, my thoughts were somewhere else. I am ashamed to say that I didn't care who was watching and as they secured the bindings to my legs, I wanted them to fail. Even as I stepped off the platform and waved, I wanted the ground to rise up and swallow me so that I could escape and forget. Now, I dread to think what effect it would have had on my watching daughter, my boys and my partner, but in that moment I was a lost cause.

44. Stigma attached.

Surviving and continuing along the same path of self-destruction, carrying the guilt of my selfish intentions with me as I travelled, I tried to increase the intensity of my workouts. Two days after the bungee jump I had finished a day shift and, feeling under the weather, decided to have an early night. The morning fitness session had been hard and despite the chesty cough and heavy cold, I had persevered. I had to complete it because my brain told me so.

The smoking may not have helped matters of course, but the fags were still my crutch, and remained a necessary evil although it was an indulgence that I knew would have to go at some point. The worries about the cigarette ash were still part of everyday life but they were a safer option than some of the more intrusive thoughts that caused so much distress and at the time, easier than quitting the habit. Some days it could take me half an hour to be satisfied that the last smoke before I left for work was absolutely dormant. That meant that the manic stubbing out and subsequent finger licking was time consuming and had no real purpose other than satisfying the urge, convincing me that I had done enough, eaten the fire that could have destroyed my family.

The children weren't staying on this particular evening but before bed I carried out the usual rituals, whilst my partner waited patiently. She knew I was under the weather and tried to help with the night-time routine, but feeling particularly troubled I spent longer than normal with light switches, doors, windows and electrical appliances.

That switch is off, not too sure, I can see that it's off but my brain doesn't understand, so I have to keep trying until I am sure. The door is locked as I have turned the key, I know I have turned the key but after a second, I am not so sure. Keep opening and closing and turning the lock until I am sure. The kettle is off, I have turned it off but now I am confused, is the switch in the correct position? I am definitely not sure, and the only way to be sure is to repeat and check and check again. These petty rituals may be some of the regular issues that lots of normal people face to a varying degree, more of an obsessive compulsive syndrome feature, so for me it really is a breeze, but tonight it feels harder than usual.

Finally in bed and trying to relax I felt a sudden pain in my chest but it went away as soon as it arrived and I managed to fall asleep more quickly than usual. The nocturnal environment is a challenging one even now and although I don't need to repeat and count and swear and pray like I did as a child, it is always a period of reflection and interrogation.

The pain hit me a few hours later and I woke with my chest feeling like I had a knife piercing my lungs. I couldn't inhale without crying out, and lying by my side my partner immediately reacted to the noise. My breathing was short and shallow and laboured because the stabbing of the knife hit home at every breath. I tried to sit and compose myself but I could not move and I was frightened.

Ten minutes later the ambulance pulled on to the drive and for the first time in my life I was a guest of an emergency vehicle and speeding my way to hospital, which fortunately for me was only five minutes away. The tumbledown cottage was a mere hop from safety and in no time I was being wheeled into the emergency department.

Some intravenous morphine eased the pain a little and at least I could introduce a little more air to my lungs but I was convinced there was something seriously wrong. Relieved, I was told it was nothing too life threatening but after two days of tests and lots of prodding, poking, injections and questioning I was diagnosed with pleurisy and double pneumonia. My lung had collapsed and there was fluid where it shouldn't have been. Soon admitted to the ward on some serious antibiotics, I was told I would recover or at least improve within a day or so but I failed to respond as expected. My white blood cells had taken over and I needed further exploratory procedures and a drain fitted to release the fluid from my lung.

Finally my condition stabilised and I was moved from the comfort of the surgical ward to a remote, prefabricated building in the original 1930's part of the hospital. Three days had passed since my admission and I felt confused because I was still terribly ill and was lying in a single-storey wooden box that had the appearance of something from a Second World War prison camp, the only difference being that the nurses had modern uniforms. There were eight beds and each was occupied by an elderly and dare I say it, infirm, individual. The nurse entered the ward and I asked politely why I was here, in this particular place surrounded by geriatric patients. 'These poor patients all appear to have some form of mental limitation so is that why I am here, because of my past?'

'Not at all,' came the response. 'It is simply that the medical ward beds have to be released for new admissions and this ward has always been a rehabilitation centre.' I found this strange as I had visited friends and family many times at the hospital during their recovery from various ailments, but never once in this section. I had also attended many false alarms in the south sector and most of the wards were either derelict or seldom used. In fact, five years later the whole area was bulldozed and earmarked for new housing.

Gradually over the next few days I got the impression that I may have misinterpreted and overreacted, as a few youngsters were moved in. I felt guilty that my suspicious nature provoked my earlier reaction and tried to make conversation with the new arrivals. Trust, or lack of it, had always been my weakness. Not entirely true in hindsight, because I remembered trusting Dad once when we were playing darts in the kitchen.

The dart board hung from a nail on the back of the kitchen door and I even had my own set of darts. I was thirteen or fourteen years old and had practised for hours, day after day. Even darts became a bit of an obsession. I didn't really like it that much either, found it really boring but sometimes I couldn't leave the board until I went 'round the clock successfully'. For the uninitiated, that is hitting each digit consecutively from number one all the way through to the bull's eye. The trouble was that with me and my insatiable need for a challenge and mind-numbing ritual, I complicated matters by having to hit the doubles and the trebles of each number before I could move on to the next. It drove me nuts with frustration but short-term pain meant long-term gain and I became quite the marksman.

Dad rated his arrows ability and had a real competitive streak. You could say that he had 'competitive dad' syndrome and he certainly had the build for a darts player. The previous few years had taken their toll on his once strapping physique and now at around the age of forty, all the hours spent at the wheel of his wagon, tramping across the country, eating all the wrong food and still combating the tedium with sixty-plus fags a day, his body had descended into rapid free fall.

He certainly looked like a darts player, a cross between Jockey Wilson and Cliff Lazarenko. Perhaps if I had known at the time the dangers he faced living such a sedentary lifestyle supplemented by fried food and the persistent inhalation of benzene, tar, ammonia, arsenic and numerous other toxic chemicals, I could have persuaded him to slow the decline. Realistically that notion is little more than wishful thinking as I guess the man was just not for changing, a male Margaret Thatcher but without the hair and the hopes of a nation resting on his shoulders.

Getting back to the matter of trust, Dad challenged me to a battle of wills and said that if I would place my hand against the board and allow him to launch three darts in my general direction, he would do the same. I had lost so much face with him on so many occasions, never quite attaining the level of machismo that he desired for his only son (I should have been a girl so the story goes), there was no way I was going to avoid this opportunity. I had lost count of the number of times he had put me in a headlock with his hugely muscled, tattooed arms clamped around my neck and urged me to try to break the hold. My pleading with him not to do this because it made me panic and feel claustrophobic fell on deaf ears. Just for the record, the arms remained like tensile steel, rock solid, a legacy from his repetitive daily workout, manually loading and unloading the wagon.

The game commenced and I reached up to the board, certain that he would err on the side of safety and launch his missiles towards the boundary. But no, the first two whistled past my ear and embedded firmly in the board a fraction away from my fingers. The third one flew past me and lo and behold straight through my finger, pinning it to the board. I think I yelled quite loudly but knew I shouldn't swear, and he helped me to remove my hand from its resting place whilst stifling a belly laugh.

It missed the bone thankfully and after binding it with an old crepe bandage I retired, tail between my legs, to my lino-floored bedroom feeling extremely sorry for myself. I wondered what the conversation had been following my departure; if Mum had said anything about common sense and his propensity for exposing me to his version of becoming-a-man activities. But I had dared and had trusted.

I learned two important lessons from the experience. Firstly, that I was ridiculously naïve to even entertain the idea that he may aim to miss and secondly, if it was an accident (which I am sure it was) he was bloody awful at darts, his skills about as sophisticated as his car repairing talents.

My untrusting gene was further awakened when I discovered that the ward's two latest arrivals, the two youngsters, were just like me. The young man, who revealed that he was seventeen years old, had taken an overdose. The young lady had attempted suicide a few years earlier. To compound my doubts, a thirty-something was admitted to the bed by the window a few days later and he was an alcoholic who had been receiving treatment for his dodgy internal organs. More stable now, he joined the motley crew in Psycho Ward Ten.

The past had caught up with us all and we were segregated. I assumed we had been 'quarantined' for our own protection, because we were vulnerable. The stigma was like '70s fly paper: you just couldn't shake it off. Ten years on, a 'normal' everyday illness and I had a large label placed around my neck. Instead of *Nil by mouth,* mine read, *Warning: serious risk of self-harm.*

45. The hovel.

Getting back to full fitness was simple for me despite the words of caution from the doctor. The benefit of physical exertion was one of my specialist subjects and now I also had medical reasons to get back in the zone. Within a couple of weeks of leaving the hospital my health had improved tremendously and I soon returned to Outpatients for a progress report. My lungs were on the mend and the prognosis supported my return to work a month later, following the standard fitness test and obligatory visit to Occupational Health.

Given the all clear, I returned to work amidst seemingly obvious concern for my mental state and as a result found myself trying to convince everyone that this had been a regular illness rather than one of those 'stress-related ones'. That was how anything that resembled a psychological issue was now being labelled. It made things far less personal, far less sinister and didn't imply that madness had struck. Some sensitive nodding, knowing glances and sympathetic sighs alerted me to the fact that perhaps my period of absence was being considered an extension of my inherent instability. Maybe I was just paranoid.

Settling back into the routine of work and tirelessly renovating the old cottage, the time slipped by rapidly.

The children still stayed over occasionally but more often than not had received better offers and would faithfully promise to see me next week or as soon as they were free. They were growing up and experiencing teenage pleasures and life at their mum's tended to be, let's say, more easy-going with fewer rules and more comforts.

I can't say I blame them with our home being a complete disaster area, progress with the renovations heavily impacted by cash flow problems and a lack of time. The maintenance payments agreed by the famed Child Support Agency were disproportionate in how they favoured one household over another and living day to day was about all we could manage. Consequently we lived in a virtual hovel for three or four years, only tackling the jobs requiring no cash input. The conditions were poor at best and my eldest refused to come and stay because she was too embarrassed about the missing staircase, the soil floors and portable toilet. Not to mention that whilst lying in bed at night with absent ceilings, you could literally see the stars through a roof that had seen better days and would require a fortune to replace.

This was all largely irrelevant to my partner and me as we shared a vision of how lovely it would look when completed and this spurred us on through the years of doubts. The added pressure also stimulated improvement in my mood as I thrived on the labour-intensive activity, and the strenuous nature of the work created a similar feel-good factor to that generated during my training sessions. A win-win situation made all the more incredible by the news that we were expecting our first child. We had not planned to increase the family but were overjoyed when our son arrived. Looking at him in his little cot next to his mother's bed in the maternity ward I dared to believe I was cured because I had no malicious thoughts, no harmful urges, only pure love and pride.

46. The new arrival.

During the days after his birth I was so excited to be a father again and the euphoria it created ran alongside my expectations of a wonderful, enlightened future. These foolish expectations were destined to be short-lived as I soon became bogged down with the same old struggles and this return to reality brought me back down to earth with a hefty bump. The extreme thoughts crept up on me within the first few days of welcoming my son home. He had been protected whilst in the womb and I realised that my wife, tired and desperate for rest after a twenty-four-hour labour needed me to assume responsibility for this tiny soul.

Memories of the early days as a new father some fourteen years earlier filled me with dread and fear and although I knew I loved him intensely, my brain wanted to convince me otherwise. He was so vulnerable and I was so alone with my thoughts, not being able to share them with anyone at that time for fear of encouraging outrage and disgust. How would my wife understand my crazy thoughts? It was one thing to accept similar compulsions aimed at non-relatives but entirely another to have one's own flesh and blood as the target.

Feeling like I wanted to destroy my own son, I didn't know how, I didn't know why, I simply felt the urge and I couldn't seem to block it out. Why would I have such thoughts when my love for him was so intense and everyone around me could plainly see that level of affection? He was more precious to us both than our own lives and my need to protect him from any kind of danger was in itself an obsession.

My brain was working against me and trying to convince me that I was deceiving myself and that all the good in me was purely a smokescreen, a web of deceit, masking my true intentions. It was irrational but it was absolutely real and despite the experiences with my older children, this was different. It felt more intense and I suspected that the constant assault, with confusing messages being processed by my overactive brain was causing my fears to intensify.

I wasn't ready for the way it made me feel. It sounds weird because I wouldn't have thought anything could have had a greater impact than the threat I had imagined myself to be to my older children and virtually anyone else that happened to be alone with me at any given time in the past.

It was all too much and completely soul-destroying. Perhaps now, because my Utopia was a perfect family unit with all relevant components rather than me and the older children against the world, my life was complete and I didn't deserve such good fortune and I was getting exactly what I deserved. Perhaps it was more to do with my inability to be a full-time dad as opposed to the weekend and special occasion variety. I was once again struggling, unable to escape from the power of my own mind, and the lure of the self-destruct button was becoming more difficult to ignore.

Part-time parenting had allowed some respite, periods alone that allowed me to recharge, to create worries outside the home to minimise the focus on my own flesh and blood. The outsiders were expendable, in theory at least: they meant less, and required less attention. Living like a proper family was clearly too much for me and I didn't know what to do about it. I began to think it may be time to run away, to do the right thing for those I loved, but I couldn't even pluck up the courage to do that. To me this was another sign of weakness and I wanted to prove that I was strong because I couldn't accept another failure.

My boy was a beautiful, blond bundle of energy, a mixture of all three older children and the likeness no doubt helped to stimulate the same harrowing obsessions and compulsions that put me away in the asylum. I should have been more prepared and more able to manage the situation with the help of my long term medication and my knowledge of the illness. Every step, every aspect of life was influenced by extracts from my colossal library of destructive memories, and they could appear from nowhere in an instant.

Was I feeding him too quickly? He could choke. The food was not properly liquidised; he could choke. He lived on baked beans mashed with a fork through a sieve because he refused to eat anything else, but I couldn't do the mashing because the husks would sometimes make him cough and I would obsess that I had deliberately failed to prepare his food safely, intending to court disaster. Pots of the stuff had to be produced in advance and it wasn't long before even that precautionary measure didn't convince me I was safe to feed him. A spoonful holding an unblended bean causing projectile vomiting must have been my fault because anyone else would have spotted the schoolboy error. They would have immediately removed the offending article.

He bumped his head and it was my fault because I should have noticed the danger. He fell off the chair because I had missed him climbing; he swallowed some fluff because I wanted him to choke and I should have picked it up before he had the opportunity. I touched the bleach and may not have washed my hands properly meaning he could die if my hands went near his face and mouth. His milk was too hot, it could burn his insides. I touched the soft spot on the crown of his head and my touch was too hard and the bones were not fused. It was deliberate. These were just the easy things, the things that I could work my way through but the real issues soon appeared, and they were a different matter because they involved weapons, violent actions and planned assaults. The nightmare was continuing and I felt powerless to fight it.

He was angelic and happy as he bounced merrily in the doorway, securely suspended in the baby harness that was clipped to the top of the doorframe. He giggled, gurgled and dribbled as I tickled him while he bounced, and I smiled, feeling the warm glow I should feel as a doting and loving father. But all the time I was having to block the evil thoughts that were threatening to poison my temporary joy as they shouldered their way into my consciousness.

47. Echoes resounding from long ago.

I remember my oldest boy at nine months, in my arms on a pleasant day at the asylum, and feeling slightly improved it was the perfect day for me to take a walk with his mum in the sprawling grounds. The moment I stepped through the huge oak door on to the steps leading to the car park I saw the cars manoeuvring in front of me. He was tiny and defenceless and as I looked into his little round face the thought that I wanted to throw him in front of a car unleashed the nausea and dread that had haunted me repeatedly. Sixty feet later and I tested myself, but passing the test wasn't enough, again and again it failed to convince me. I felt evil, scared, desperate, sick and monstrous. I handed him over and went back to my bed and cried.

Now facing the same challenges with a different bundle of joy, I tried to focus on the fact that I had never acted on any of my thoughts and that surely meant that I was a safe pair of hands. I wanted to use logic and common sense to ignore the irrational thoughts, maybe allow them fleeting recognition, and move on quickly. This wouldn't work because if I failed to face the threat and prove myself, it meant that I had accepted the consequences of inactivity and virtually invited disaster. What I mean is that to not tackle a compulsion is the same as committing the act.

A simple example would be failing to pick up all the fluff from the carpet. The decision to fight the compulsion and ignore the urge would leave me with a worse dilemma. The fluff would be appealing to the child, the child would pick it up and place it in the place where young children tend to place everything, but the child survives, he doesn't choke. In my head that would be irrelevant as the decision to ignore the risk had been made. My mind would interpret the failure to act as a deliberate attempt to cause harm. Had I collected the fluff using some obsessional, time consuming ritual I may have allowed myself to feel OK.

The cycle could not be broken, but I knew I couldn't carry on like this. I didn't want to give up and so I decided to embrace some of my rituals and obsessions rather than fighting them. I hoped it would help me avoid some of the more sinister compulsions. My biggest decision. however, was to believe and trust in my family.

Surprisingly I began to see a difference, not necessarily easier but I handled it a little better. I was less inclined to panic, to curl up into a ball like a hedgehog hiding from a predator. I started the process by carrying my son as often as I could, because I knew that the alternative was equally as challenging. The buggy could easily be pushed into the path of an approaching vehicle so it was a no-win situation. The anxiety, the nervous perspiration, the excruciating wait until the car had passed, the need for the next car to appear to ensure I was doubly sure, presented the same internal disgust and fear. Then came an unfamiliar response, an ability to occasionally walk away and save the test for another day. It didn't happen often and the initial feeling was usually one of emptiness and unfinished business, but the emotional part of my brain would quickly offer up the next dilemma, leaving no room to ponder missed opportunities. Perhaps in a chaotic way I was learning a strategy.

Swimming trips presented enormous problems for me because the vulnerability and innocence of this tiny form in the buoyancy aid was all my brain needed to associate fun times with my earliest memories of sinking below the surface, my life fading away. He giggled and kicked and waved his chubby arms but even with my heart bursting with love it wasn't enough to prevent the wicked intentions resurfacing. The four-year-old who had nearly drowned so long ago, had left his legacy.

Years before, with three children in the pool it was impossible to isolate one in order to create the danger in my head, but with one small dependant I had little choice but to consider my ability to protect or harm. I was occasionally able to manage the threat by using the avoidance tactics I had devised, delaying the trial for another day when my mind was better suited to the challenge. On occasions when I was taken by surprise and thrust into a life or death situation it still destroyed me but I coped somehow.

Now that those days are long gone and the children all have far greater independence I ask myself the question, 'How could anyone drown a child in a pool full of people?' The answer is 'with difficulty', and most people would consider the idea an immature fantasy. That may be true but even nowadays when joined by my adult and teenage children in a sun-kissed holiday pool, relaxed and relieved because they are all competent swimmers, I still face deep-seated fears. Generated by a misplaced hand, a poorly secured stopper in an inflatable or neglect of a duty to protect, the fear of being instrumental in a fatality will never leave me. But I think I may be able to live with it, I have to because it is part of me.

48. Premature disaster.

The terrible guilt and self-loathing I still feel when I think about how OCD impacted on my relationship with the older children will always trouble me. There is no doubt that they had lots of love and cuddles from me on those special weekends but I missed out on so much of their childhood. Gradually I saw less and less of them, the two boys in particular, as their home life was every teenager's dream, free to come and go as they pleased and allowed every opportunity to exploit that freedom to the extreme.

Sad and disappointed that I had insufficient ammunition to inspire greater contact, my eldest son who is now twenty eight with two daughters of his own, once hadn't stayed with us for almost six months. We spoke on the telephone quite regularly and I would stand on the touchline watching his weekend football matches but apart from that we spent no time together.

His football was everything to him, and it brought back fond memories of my early years, hammering the old leather case ball against the wall, anticipating the sound of Dad bellowing through the walls at me. Years later during weekend visits, we would spend hours in the garden with me usually keeper, between the scaffold pole goals I had erected, as he flicked and swerved the ball, making me look a fool as I dived the wrong way or stood motionless as the ball flew past my ears. Far more talented than I had ever been, he really had something.

Preparing to leave for work one Monday morning the telephone rang and I was told to get to the hospital as soon as I could. Whilst eating his breakfast before leaving for school my son had suffered some kind of seizure and was now receiving emergency treatment, seriously ill with a panic-stricken mother screeching down the phone at me. I didn't wait to press for details and raced to the hospital, fearing the worst.

He had always been a slightly built child and hadn't had a great start in life, appearing six weeks before full term, thirteen years earlier. He had been the cause of considerable concern during the last few months of the pregnancy, prompting numerous extra visits to maternity and an assortment of tests that fortunately all proved to be normal. Just a lazy baby, they said, his future potential as a footballer not yet apparent.

Within minutes of the unexpected arrival I held him in my arms and stared at his tiny form, quickly noticing something strange. Was it strange or was it my mind playing tricks on me? He didn't look right, his colour was all wrong and my habit over the years of listening intently for breathing patterns and signs of a moving chest, was telling me I needed to call out. I told myself not to panic, unsure of my observations and concluding that I was the stereotypical father of a new arrival, shocked and delirious with excitement and pride.

Seconds later I was convinced that I couldn't see his chest move, couldn't hear him breathe. His face colouring looked fairly normal, pinkish and not too pale but could that be the aggressive artificial lighting and the mass of black hair conspiring to deceive me? Then he looked bluer or was it purple, colour seeming to change in every anxious second but was I going to make a fool of myself, the panicky new dad?

No, I wasn't wrong. 'Nurse, nurse, there's something wrong, I can't hear him breathe!' She strode up to me and it took the briefest of looks to decide what to do. She snatched him from my arms and pressed the alarm button, disappearing from the room in a flash. I was immediately distraught, I had delayed for reasons of pride, I had waited ten, perhaps twenty seconds before raising the alarm and that may be the difference between my first son's life and death. I realised I had probably just killed my son, not deliberately; or was it? Surely someone with my experience ought to have seen the signs and acted on impulse and not been concerned about what people would think if the hunch had been wrong.

We waited for what seemed like a lifetime, not speaking or hugging, simply hanging there, anticipating the loss of this tiny premature baby and it was all my fault. This couldn't be OCD talking, this was reality and I had finally gone and done it. I was absolutely right, I was mad and the evidence was just about to present itself to the world.

The doctor returned and provided us, me in particular, with the best news of my life. He was OK, in an incubator, resuscitated and on oxygen, but alive. The drama was over, apart from some special care and a few weeks in the transparent box with wires and tubes everywhere, providing his weak little body with extra help.

My guilt increased day by day during two weeks of wondering if whilst touching his tiny, dry little fingers and his soft, innocent face, I had inadvertently (or otherwise) displaced one of the life support systems. I had to check each connection over and over again until I could convince myself that his lifelines were secure whilst all the time hoping that I wouldn't be discovered. Should someone appear mid-ritual they would consider me odd at best and at worst, heaven knows. They could accuse me of sabotage, why else would I be tampering in that manner?

My intentions were genuine but the interruption would trigger the paranoia, the self-defeating terror. I knew why I needed to interfere but I would struggle to defend myself given the doubts in my own head, and with no independent witnesses my fate would be sealed.

Now thirteen years on and in the hospital ward, the bay was buzzing with people; he was crying with pain but I couldn't listen. He was a young man being manipulated and probed by an assortment of professionals but I was in a complete daze. I tried to find out what was wrong with him and nobody could tell me for sure. His mum was still there and she said that it may be linked to meningitis, while a nurse said, 'We just don't know but it seems it was some kind of fit or seizure.'

I must have looked a mess because I was told to leave, to take a seat in the family room where I was advised that all would be fine. I retreated to the smoking canopy where I lit up, tears rolling down my cheeks, and without fear of embarrassment I cried out loud.

The next day once again very little information was available; he couldn't speak, smile or move. I stood with my mother, my wife and sisters in the waiting room waiting for news, any news, but it failed to materialise. I broke down again, my emotions all over the place. My fears for his future were complicated by guilt once again because this must have been my fault. All those years ago in the Special Care baby unit, it was my inability to react quickly to obvious danger signals and my continuing failure to be a proper father. It was one of the lowest points in my entire life.

49. Stroke.

Four long days of anxious waiting, pacing the corridors, and hours of questioning my part in all of this made me realise that the illness currently threatening my own flesh and blood gave everyone all the evidence they needed in order to see, hear, touch and sense his suffering. They could empathise and sympathise and understand the reality of it all.

My family all reacted in different ways, some stronger than others, quietly crying in private, me with my heart on my sleeve, baring the raw emotion without shame and not conscious of the impact it may have on the rest. Mental illness, on the other hand, provides little of that information and I have no doubt that the lack of evidence is why society establishes its own rules and allows the negativity to endure. Physical proof is so much easier to believe and to understand.

Several scans and neurological investigations later, they finally concluded that my thirteen- year-old had suffered a major stroke. More often than not an episode associated with those of an advanced age, the diagnosis had been delayed. Why was that so? No firm answers were provided but I gathered there was no shame in failing to suspect a fit, intelligent and exuberant teenager would have succumbed to this potentially catastrophic assault on his brain.

The damage was plain to see on the scan pictures, an area of dead tissue, the shape and size of a large chicken's egg. My boy had been lucky and his age and fitness had combined to minimise the impact. In the short-term a seriously ill young man, but mercifully a long-term survivor.

Because of his youthfulness, his recovery was remarkable and within three months he was walking and talking as if nothing had happened. With the aid of a word processor he was able to return to school and continue with his education. He was unable to write for around twelve months as his left side retained some physical incapacity and unfortunately he was left handed. He failed to do the recommended physiotherapy that would help to rehabilitate the problems with his left arm and this resulted in a slight amount of permanent damage and although not obvious to most, I see a left hand clenched lightly as a fist hanging loosely from a less developed and slightly limp left arm. He has no regrets, no fears, is completely laid back and completely happy with his simple existence and the pressures of the world rarely graze the surface of his personality. Humbling and enlightening to witness, I often wish I could be so content.

The guilt I was feeling almost drove me to distraction and I can honestly say that without support I would have continued to wallow in desperation. To this day I remain convinced that I should have picked up the birth breathing problems a few seconds earlier, vital seconds that could have made all the difference to my son's future. That critical mistake still haunts me but with the constant tide of so many other negatives it only threatens when a space appears in my consciousness and when the more recent issues have been suitably dealt with. Perhaps I should cut myself some slack but my mind does not allow that kind of forgiveness. Not yet at least.

50. New life, brings new challenges.

The birth of my second daughter soon after my son's miraculous recovery enabled me to focus on something other than past guilt and historical harmful thoughts once again: two youngsters and recycled thought processes from years ago when my first family was in its infancy kept me teetering on the survival tightrope.

Moving further into my forties at an alarming rate I couldn't help thinking that my life, or at least any potentially good parts of it were passing me by without ever providing me with any real satisfaction. I felt like I was living in a dream world and that I was forever looking in at myself, analysing and picking apart everything I had ever done, worrying about the present day and anticipating the next helping of trouble lurking in the shadows.

Thirty or more years of OCD had worn me down and although I was extremely happy with my new family, somehow it was never enough to put a spring in my step. I awoke every single day with the same desperation, the same disabling feeling of sickness in the pit of my stomach and my mind and body unable to feel real happiness. I longed for some inspiration, just a little taste of something that would prove I wasn't mad and that I was improving and learning to live. In the old days I would have resorted to extra marital interaction but on this occasion I decided instead to try a mid-life crisis of sorts, to try and ease the pain.

A new and more powerful motorbike fitted the bill as it would give me an ideal opportunity to lose myself once in a while and allow me to forget my problems. With a twist of the throttle I would be propelled towards a new sunset and closer to a more positive future. The theory sounded good but it hadn't worked for the past ten years or so with my previous machines, although they had all been old and decrepit and solely a means of transport. My new machine would be a toy, something sleek and pristine and entirely for pleasure.

A couple of rapid promotions at work and the reduction in the payments demanded by the Child Support Agency, as we now had children of our own, provided an increase in disposable income. Combined with a hastily arranged remortgage we could afford a holiday and a new two-wheeled crisis buster. Not just for me you understand, as my wife also loved the thrill of speed and the freedom of the road.

Chances to get away were few and far between with two youngsters to consider, but when it came down to it, maternal instinct and the inherent danger associated with modern day, two-wheeled transport, meant I had to go it alone on my quest for enlightenment. She had made a good call too, as my level of irresponsibility knew no bounds. It was far too easy to don the leather gear and helmet and to ease my frustrations by hitting the roads with pure abandon and not nearly enough natural skill. The risks were plainly seen by everyone, except me! Depression and stupidity do not form a happy partnership, and hunched over the fuel tank, oblivious to anything other than self-fulfilment, I used the bike as an escape from reality.

One such jaunt too many and the inevitable happened. Country roads, rain-swept gravel from the previous day's downpour washed from verge to the carriageway and a bump and slide into oblivion. I lay motionless on the road waiting for someone to come along to scrape me up, not aware of my good fortune. No brick walls, other road vehicles, or road furniture with which to collide, just some pain, a kindly motorist and a fifteen-minute wait at the side of the road.

The ambulance had been some thirty minutes away but I had been out for the count. They loaded me on to the ambulance, and through the open back doors I glimpsed my pride and joy lying in a crumpled mess at the side of the road some fifty metres away. I felt some relief that it had ended its journey near a gateway and was not creating a hazard to other road users. My conscience was clear. Morphine once again administered to ease the pain in my arm, foot and ribs, slightly numbed the multitude of thoughts cluttering my brain as I was transported back along the roads I had travelled a short while earlier.

I was sickened by my foolishness and I tried to recall the feelings that had influenced my stupidity. On the surface I had a life that would satisfy any man and I remembered many times when people had said to me that my life was so perfect. They didn't need to tell me that I had everything anyone could reasonably wish for: a beautiful home, a beautiful wife, five healthy and intelligent children and a great job in which I had been able to achieve a great deal. They would shake their heads and ask, 'What have you got to be depressed about?' They just didn't get it. How could they understand?

Naturally I could never own up and tell the truth about my inner secrets because it would just confirm I was exactly that which I was trying so hard to hide from society. I would usually talk about the things that had hurt me in the past and pretend that I worried too much about simple things. One of my fallback options was to explain that I was struggling to come to terms with my ex finally owning up to the paternity issue after so many years of denial.

Despite being exonerated, it was difficult for a man to admit that his young cousin had violated the 'sanctity' of his marriage. The boy was now ten or eleven years old and even he knew now that I was not the heartless human being he had been led to believe. You could get away with telling such secrets as people always love a scandal and the bonus is that they may actually have sympathy for you too. I didn't know if the other children cared a great deal but I was convinced that my eldest had always believed her mother.

I talked about how I had confronted her one day many years ago and had begged her to tell the truth. She had queried my intentions and I explained that I knew the new baby was perhaps genetically linked to me but was not actually mine. She said again that I was delusional and that she could hurt me more than I could ever imagine, but I reminded her that I could no longer be hurt. I had moved on. I told her to be honest and tell the children about their brother's heritage and their father's innocence.

Her words had stayed with me, etched in my grey matter like an ever-present stain. The acid tongue that had always found a way to press my buttons responded, 'One of them not yours? More like three of them!'

Just before the ride I had been mulling over the difficulties I had faced the previous evening as we put the two little ones to bed. My worries about cot death had triggered many return visits to their rooms to check on their breathing and to make sure that the covers had not found a way of impeding their airways. This was a legacy from the maternity ward nightmare and was a constant problem for me. The dilemma of how a baby should be laid to sleep had always raised considerable debate amongst professionals. On this occasion I had struggled to leave because my brain would not accept that all was well.

I spent close to an hour in one room, bending and listening, walking to the door and returning once again, my ear getting ever closer to the child. If I touched the covers or a hair on the head with any part of my face it would have to be done all over again. I held my breath to create the silence I needed so as not to miss the faintest sound. I looked for the slightest movement of the fabric, the hint that the chest was rising and falling, but no matter what my eyes and ears told me, my brain refused to co-operate.

This particular evening my wife had to drag me away. She knew me well and saved me from further torture by assuring me that both were safe and well, at the same time as preventing another meltdown. I had briefly believed that the fear of my harming the children had been banished but I was wrong, it hadn't. I had tested and tested until I was exhausted and had achieved nothing. Her intervention had saved me but also filled me with self-hatred because I had failed to convince myself, but of what, I do not know. I resolved to do something that I had sworn I would never have to do again. I needed help, I needed a psychiatrist.

Many years had passed since the asylum but the realisation that professional help was the only answer reminded me of some chilling words spoken by an ex-relative at the time. Never my biggest fan she uttered, 'Once he has been in there, he will be in and out like a yo-yo.' That was never going to happen; I couldn't let it happen. For some it may be the only solution but for me it would be the end of the road. So I just hopped on the bike and sped off the driveway.

She was absolutely correct of course, although not in the context she had predicted. The asylum for us in the service was one of the most frequently attended premises during the nineties and early noughties as they suffered numerous Automatic Fire Alarm activations and were also prone to attempts by residents to set the place ablaze by igniting the litter bins.

The first few visits were stressful to say the least, as old memories came flooding back leaving me wondering if someone would recognise me and approach me, destroying any credibility I had been able to regain with my colleagues. Perhaps the fact that I seemed to know my way around the place meant that my cover had already been blown but it still took a number of years before I was able to enter the main reception area without a certain amount of apprehension. Truthfully, that is a huge understatement as I felt pure dread, stimulated by the sights, sounds, and smells of the past.

51. Trepidation.

By the time the appointment with the psychiatrist arrived I needed to take some time off work. The doctor whom I had not seen before had signed me off for a month, purely because my file indicated a history of mental illness and a month appeared to be the norm. It seemed to me that general practitioners often had scant knowledge of mental illness and that their philosophy was this default solution, giving a patient time to improve whilst removing the need to make decisions or plan an appropriate course of action. That was the way I saw it anyway. I likened it to suffering a musculoskeletal injury where, without exception, the physical nature of my occupation would dictate a six-week sabbatical without consideration of specific roles within the organisation. It felt like a tick in the box.

Having not spoken to outsiders about the extent of my intrusive thoughts for so many years, I had real concerns about how my crazy confessions would be viewed. I realised that I had no choice but was convinced that at some point I would be confined to a room with a bespectacled, bearded professional who would show me pictures and ask what I saw, leading him to assess the extent of my madness. He would talk about the thoughts and try to establish their origins and maybe even get an introduction to an invisible special friend.

Supported by my wife I entered the room with great trepidation and sat in front of a huge oak desk, behind which was seated a rather friendly looking Sikh gentleman. He was very familiar and I soon realised that I had seen him regularly in his big Mercedes estate car on roads near home. Living in an area that is not renowned for its ethnic diversity, his bright orange turban was instantly recognisable.

What a nice man! I thought as he spoke to me with his soft, deep tones, sweetened further by the faintest hint of an Indian accent. He could see that I was nervous and made a point of telling me that he had read my notes and was familiar with OCD, and in particular the intrusive nature of my thoughts.

I explained that I hated talking about my problems and that it often lowered my mood further if certain aspects were raised. He asked me to talk about my experiences and feelings from the point of waking in the morning to going to bed at night and specifically how different situations impacted my thoughts and how my thoughts impacted simple daily routines and activities. This was going to be difficult but I could sense his wisdom and experience and had a good feeling about him. That always helps, a positive start to the day.

I felt I needed a safety net just in case he deceived me, actually intending to lock me away. I explained that I didn't get depressed every day, and that many rituals were just part of me now and I hardly noticed them. I stressed that the most troubling events were exceptions. I wasn't sure if I was being completely honest but then again, how would I know? With a history like mine, how could I understand honesty when making sure I kept my freedom was the only objective?

52. A bad day in the life.

I wake for what seems like the hundredth time, but now it's time for work, the feeling deep inside my head is something I find hard to describe. The only comparison I can make is to say it's like a heavy weight compressing my brain and squeezing out any sign of happiness. It takes me an age to lift my sleep-deprived body from the bed and step into the day.

The children have not yet stirred but my thoughts immediately focus on them. Today, once again, I cannot summon the confidence to enter their rooms to check on them. I go to the door and call because I know that now is not the time to face my demons. At least I have learned something. As Dr Peters says, you cannot control the chimp in you, you can only learn to manage it.

They both wake and now I can approach and give each of them a big hug and a good morning kiss. Because they are no longer asleep the risk is reduced and although I still feel edgy as I embrace them, the evil thoughts are in the back of my mind. Difficult to explain what the thoughts are, but I sense that something is lurking just beyond consciousness.

If my wife happens to enter the room at the wrong time, the doubts will surface, leaving me wondering if my actions could have been more sinister had she not appeared. She needs to leave the room, and only then can I achieve peace of mind by repeating the greeting without the risk of disturbance.

Off to the bathroom for a wash. I must make sure that the taps are turned off properly before I leave. Why? I don't know, but my brain tells me there is a risk and if I ignore the signal I may as well just give up now. You have to understand that even though my normal self tells me that a dripping tap offers no danger, my compulsion is to check and check again, because to fail to comply would indicate a lack of care and thus an intention to cause harm.

The bathroom light doesn't click off properly, it makes a noise that just isn't quite right. I need to do it again and again until it sounds right. The landing light doesn't click off properly, it also makes the wrong noise, so I have to repeat the action until it feels right. Wait, I think there was a spark from the switch. I will be leaving for work and that spark may mean disaster after I have left. Possibly an inferno due to an electrical fault. The entire family will be in peril and it will be my fault because I saw the tell-tale sign and failed to act. I switch it on and off several times until my eyes don't see what my brain is telling me. It must be my senses playing games again because there is no spark and I can safely go downstairs.

Downstairs for breakfast and the dogs greet us with the usual excitement, the unconditional affection and fuss that one seldom receives from humans. My porridge goes in the microwave but I have to make sure that my fingers are bone dry after my wash, before I flick the switch. Damp hands may lead to a problem later in the day when I am not around to protect my family, It can be difficult to satisfy myself that the finger I use is dry enough, so a few cycles of wiping the digit on my shirt and then perhaps on the skin on my neck to remove any fibres that have adhered to it from the shirt before I carefully depress the switch. If I touch any other part of the socket or plug, I must repeat the procedure until I make no mistakes.

The kettle boils and I pour my coffee and a cup of tea for my wife. Without exception a quantity of condensed steam and a few stray drops of water gather after dripping down the side of the kettle. I can't put it back on the element until I have wiped the rim with my spare hand, but now that is wet too and I am unable to dry it completely. I am now stranded with a dangerous appliance in my hand. If I return it to its base there's a possibility that water will seep into the element and create a risk to those left at home. What the risk is, I don't really know but I just can't ignore the thought because it is so powerful that it makes my heart beat faster and teases beads of sweat from my brow.

My shoes need cleaning, so I rummage around in the cupboard beneath the kitchen sink for the polish, brushes and the cloth that will enhance the shine. The black, greasy, petroleum-based paste smears on to my forefinger as I brush and I think of the hazard this will create if I don't spend more than an inordinate amount of time to remove it. So I wash my hands several times to show that I have done everything within my power to remove or at least reduce the risk. I notice a plastic bottle marked with an X in the cupboard as I put the cleaning gear away and recognising that the letter stands for danger I try to avoid the bleach, carelessly touching the lid in my haste to complete my routine.

I need to wash my hands again and as I do so, I recall times gone by when bleach was one of my worst fears. I worried that the children could come into contact with it, causing catastrophic injuries because of course they would be sure to try to drink it and by simply touching this caustic solution they would suffer horrific burns. Some of my concerns were alleviated when a kind soul poured a few drops on one of my toddler son's favourite books one day and showed me how clean and undamaged it was once he had wiped it away. For a few days it sounded feasible, until I remembered that it was the intent rather than the risk that caused the problems and so now, years later, the danger has returned. Ironic when you think that Obsessional Compulsive cleaners use it like water and they never seem to care but then again, they don't understand the danger.

Maybe today I can escape and get to the office on time, where no one knows about the tests I have already passed. If in doubt I can rely on my wife to reassure me that all is well before I leave. When worried about my actions or lack of action causing harm she is happy to be my personal relief valve. Sometimes the reassurance makes things worse because next time I will need that little bit more of it to allow me to emerge from the cycle. This is a bad day so I have to think of an excuse for being late.

Relieved, I sit in the car and look back at the window where they all wave and smile as they watch me leave. The cottage sits in a difficult spot near the traffic island and it is a struggle to see clearly as I pull out inch by inch. There is traffic speeding past and workers and students make their way into town along the footpath obscured by the wall to my right. I have to make sure that my feet stay on the brake and the clutch as the slope of the ground tempts the car to roll forwards. I wait and listen whilst leaning toward the windscreen, all the time having fears as to whether my brain will encourage me to accelerate into some innocent passerby. I smile as someone puts their hand up to thank me for being cautious. Phase One is complete.

Now I am on my way and I start to wonder if my wife still loves me or if the constant pressure is driving a wedge between us. My behaviour must be like psychological abuse, torture, but I try harder to push it from my mind because I would be lost without her. The tension must be driving her to distraction but she always perseveres. The rehearsed actions, statements and rituals are a daily event until my mind becomes satisfied, allowing me to press on, to face and deal with more serious issues.

53. Standard practice.

Driving through the town I see people rushing to and from their places of work, the gym, an early morning coffee, and mums and dads holding hands with their toddlers excitedly making their way to nursery. My brain may alert me to the danger of the baby buggy being pushed too close to the kerb's edge and on a bad day I will think I have clipped someone and have to look in the rear view mirror to confirm they have survived.

On very bad days the sinister part of my brain convinces me that I want to bump up on to the footpath and career into some poor, unsuspecting family. I have to tense my arms and stare at the road ahead, not allowing the urges to get the better of me. Steering in the opposite direction, towards the white line, I know they have been lucky this time. When I arrive at work I feel sickened by my evil intentions.

The feeling of dread is still very much in my mind as I sit at my desk. Rarely will the clouds have moved on, but by necessity I have to settle into work mode, focusing intently on the job in hand, because how else can I convince everyone that I am a normal human being? My obsessions will have to wait until later.

Breaking from work, I walk along the corridor to the washroom. The carpet is stained and threadbare and I wonder if I am somehow contaminating the bottom of my shoes. What does it matter? Well, I have two small children and I must make sure that my shoes don't soil the carpet this evening when I get home. You never know what harmful substances could be deposited.

The cubicles are both showing red for engaged on the handles but they are not occupied so I nudge the door on the left with my foot, as I think about the many soiled hands that have touched the handle or the face of the door. Deftly manoeuvring, I kick the door shut and with an agility that comes with years of practice I slide the lock across with the same foot, balancing on one leg like a stork. I prefer to consider myself as something of a short, bald Bruce Lee or Jackie Chan.

When at home I have to sit to relieve myself no matter what the function because I worry about the unseen spray that can emanate into places you would not imagine. You can see it sometimes but only if the sun shines directly on to the stream. That said I cannot do that at work because the environment is unclean and even without considering my extreme personal standards, people do have some pretty disgusting bathroom habits.

If ever I have to sit down I place tissue over the entire seat and into the bowl. I must not touch the dispenser because of unseen germs and I have to lift and lower the seat with a foot or a triple-tissue-protected hand. Further gymnastics manage the flush and the door lock once I have relieved myself and sometimes if I feel particularly agile I stay on one leg to complete the two actions. I reach up as high as possible to pull the door inwards to allow my exit but only when I know the coast is clear. I know most people hold the door at around waist height so it should be safe.

Now it is time to wash hands but the taps have been touched by careless patrons so I use a paper towel to turn on the hot water. Not the perfect solution as they have been lying next to the sink and could be contaminated with splashes or worse, but what choice do I have? Making sure I have only pressed the soap dispenser with my knuckle I carefully wash every part of my hands without making contact with the sink. After rinsing the soap off completely I karate kick the tap to the off position with the ever-reliable right foot because clean hands cannot be allowed to touch the risky paper towels.

I can move over to the hand dryer now. There are no problems with this part of the procedure as the device comes on automatically. If I touch the metal of the dryer or make contact with the wall, I have to return to the sink and wash again. Timing is key to success, and in the event that someone should interrupt the sequence, I must temporarily vacate the room, only to return when the coast is clear for a fresh attempt to become germ free. Funnily enough I got caught mid-hop the other day and had to turn towards the dryer in embarrassment. I am not sure if he caught sight of the foot as it made contact with the tap or during its transition to the floor but I suspect there is now one civilian worker who is questioning my sanity. To be perfectly honest, I no longer care.

Holding the very top of the door handle, in a position where I hope it is less likely to have been contaminated I throw the door open to avoid any other part of my body coming into contact with it. Door handles are notoriously dangerous because humans are irresponsible when considering the risks of cross contamination. Opening the door to the office I head straight for the antiseptic gel that has been provided since the latest norovirus outbreak, or was it the avian flu pandemic? I am not entirely sure but there is always plenty available as most of my colleagues are oblivious to the risks. Should I tell them that they are walking a very thin line between life and death?

The problem is that people are noticing that I always reach for the gel and when mine runs out, their faces tell me that they are suspicious of how many times I need to borrow some. I tend to joke about OCD but of course that is fine because it's a cleaning thing or a hoarding thing or maybe a need for order and routine. Nobody seems to mind or even be the slightest bit shocked because they tend to say, 'Don't most people have a bit of that? I have a thing for stirring my tea ten times,' or, 'I often return to check that the front door is locked before I leave home,' or, 'I have to avoid the cracks in the paving slabs.' It's OK for them; it's normal to have a bit of OCD.

The small kitchen along the corridor is a minefield with everything a safe haven for germs and filth. I have to sterilise mugs and spoons with the water from the boiler before I make a drink for my colleagues. I often scald my fingers because the water overflows during my attempts to decontaminate the rim of the mug. The spoons are tarnished, meaning they need the same treatment. The bin is filthy but the paper towels come in handy. I have never lifted the lid of the bin without double towel protection. I don't bother concealing this act these days as too many people have seen through the glass panel in the door but I don't care because it's only a little compulsion. It's a race to get through the door as I only want to touch the top of the handle once. The self-closing device allows me just enough time to pick up the tray or the mugs and slip through the gap.

The office environment is a different world for me after twenty years of life on the Watch. I miss the camaraderie and the adrenalin buzz of anticipation as we hurtled off in the red engine, never knowing what we may face on arrival. To some extent I even miss the Breathing Apparatus Challenge as it was in some strange way a positive compulsion for me. Deep down it made me feel that I was reliable, safe, had always followed the rules and never failed in my duty. My concern for the next user was the priority and that must have been a good sign.

The need for a change and the lure of those fabled greener pastures propelled me into a different world. Perhaps it was the familiar itchy feet, the 'butterfly effect' recognised so many years before. I used to think my desire to move up the proverbial ladder was based on the need for self-fulfilment, a better quality of life for my family and linked to the hierarchy of human needs, as documented over the years by respected psychologists. However, my suspicion is that my propensity for never being quite satisfied has more to do with my brain chemicals and their affinity with obsession.

The regular promotions may not have rewarded me with a greater desire to get out of my bed in the morning but at least now during working hours I have fewer reasons to worry about others. Dealing with people, performance, discipline and service delivery in my day job provides stimulating yet unfamiliar challenges. I didn't join the service to sit at a desk but I now have the best of both worlds. The pager beeps and I jump in my car and, with blues and twos activated, can still reap the benefits of the rush of adrenalin, the anticipation and nervous energy stimulated by the unknown.

I ask myself how anyone with such a troubled mind can be permitted to hold a position of responsibility? Surely it requires characteristics consistent with those of a normal person, qualities such as confidence, resilience, consistency, calmness, common sense and empathy; the list goes on and on. Based on my previous confessions you are excused for failing to pick me as an obvious candidate for Emergency Services' Personality Of The Year. You may well ask how I have lasted this long. You may find it hard to believe but the truth is simple: I am usually normal.

54. Reliable me.

The modern operational environment for me is a mixture of Command and Control, Safety and Risk Management and applying practical solutions to dynamic and often challenging situations. OCD has had no opportunity to encroach on this aspect of my life because I somehow shield my brain from its disruptive and destructive tendencies.

With so much to consider, the cognitive and analytical processes that support operational decision making don't allow peripheral thoughts to interfere. No longer needing to get my hands dirty, the real action is beyond my reach, thus reducing the opportunity for OCD to interfere and get a foothold. I can save the dubious and deluded stuff until later. I can't imagine how I would feel if I had been unable to continue with my chosen career but perhaps I am still around because it was simply the right path for me.

The National Occupational Standards for Fire and Rescue Services[4] are stringent, measuring competency and performance through assessment and scrutiny, so I can reassure the normal people that they can relax because I

---

[4] Skills for Justice National Occupational Standard (NOS), EFSM2 - Lead, Monitor and Support people to resolve operational incidents.

can be trusted. I guess I am a little like Mr Benn from the '70s children's programme when I become the epitome of the uniform I wear. Not a superhero, but a man keen to enjoy an adventure, only to make a quick return to normality, wherever that place may be.

Sadly for me, but not so for the wider community, the adventures are few and far between because as one climbs the 'ladder of success', the more serious incidents requiring a higher level of management are increasingly rare. With continual developments in public safety standards and community education, I wait in the wings, just in case.

Once the working day is done, it's time for my daily fix to get my juices flowing, to sweat out any fears before they have the chance to take root today. Straight to the gym for a demanding session of circuit training or a run up the hills in the park. Sometimes my running partner and I will carry each other uphill, until we can barely breathe and our legs stubbornly refuse to carry us further.

We both use the exercise for the psychological benefits as well as the physical, but we don't talk about the underlying reasons. It is a private thing and he is manly and proud. He copes without medication because he can. I sometimes think I am weak because I don't have that kind of strength. He manages to inspire me and push me to exceed my own expectations. He says I have the physique of a man in his twenties, but he knows my face betrays the illusion, because it displays the wear and tear of reality.

I feel good, my body is exhausted but I really sense that the effort has somehow enhanced my well-being. I can't put my finger on it but it's like I am smiling on the inside and my brain is allowing some sunshine into my soul again. Very difficult to categorise the cause of this upturn in spirits and I cannot confess to know all the answers but

I thrive on the belief that the exercise is the key. I am convinced that it tops up the serotonin and dopamine tanks and flushes my toxic thoughts away and enhances the body's natural defence systems. I believe in the chemical cure and in some ways I have to because it is my holy grail, my life blood. I still don't know if my depression causes an increase in my OCD, especially the soul destroying scary episodes, or if falling into the OCD hamster wheel stimulates deeper depression. The clever scientist types also have an enigma to crack, because despite all the research they have yet to decide if a decreased serotonin level leads to depression or if depression results in a decreased serotonin level. They are certain, however, that an imbalance of such neurotransmitters can cause depression and I would vouch for increasing them every time.

The day has been long but it has been a good one and it gets even better as the children greet me with the same enthusiasm as always. I kiss my wife and I wonder how she puts up with this daily routine, the extended hours and that toss of a coin that will dictate my mood. She knows that if the day has been difficult I will need her support to help me through to bedtime. Today she will feel loved and cherished, the children will go to sleep after an evening of cuddles and positive interaction with a dad happy in the knowledge that he is the luckiest man alive. Tonight I will rest with a smile on my face. Yes, today has been a good day and I will fall asleep with ease, thinking happy thoughts and maybe even looking forward to tomorrow.

55. Do I have to tell?

Why is it that the nice doctors all speak softly? Is that a common trait or is it my imagination and an imperfect memory? Is it my want that a soft and gentle voice and calming bedside manner means that I am in safe hands and no matter what I say, they are on my side?

He broke the silence and thanked me for being open and honest about my worries but reminded me that I had ended the theoretical day on a high. He asked me if I was able to share the worst of my fears, the ones that drive me to the point of despair. I recognised that the man with the orange turban just wanted me to admit to my crimes and I could imagine the fate that awaited me as my wife encouraged me to come clean. Perhaps she, too, after all this time and constant pressure, felt that it was the right time for me to be placed in a more secure environment, so that she and the children would not be frightened for their lives. Perhaps her unrelenting support had been feigned to get me to this place. The doubts entering my head multiplied and merged into a huge ball of mistrust and I wished I hadn't exposed myself to this inquisition.

The insecure Oliver was frightened for his life but the caring, sensitive and overtly honest Oliver, the serial confessor, usually to events over which he has no control, knew that the only way to protect his family was to expose the real monster that lurked just below the surface. He knew that to renege on his responsibilities would be deceitful, and it would ultimately come back to haunt him. Once and for all it would be hard evidence that he could not be trusted and his sinister thoughts were just the tip of the iceberg. He was deliberately trying to hide the genuine evil that had been dormant for decades.

I politely asked if he has read all of my notes and seen the evidence for himself, the details from all those years ago when I was so vulnerable and frightened that I didn't care, I had just needed a safe haven. He nodded and smiled and assured me that he understood my anxiety but he needed me to explain so that he had first-hand knowledge of my current frame of mind.

I looked over at my wife and saw immediately in her eyes that this wasn't a trap, it wasn't an ambush, and she was still prepared to be my saviour, the only person in the world I could really trust. I held her hand and took a deep breath to force a bad day from my lips.

The less hectic times are often the worst as I struggle to occupy my mind, I have always known that I need to keep busy, to challenge my brain to squeeze more in, to learn more, do more, worry more. The day has an air of doom and gloom hanging over it as I wearily climb out of bed. Stepping into a psychological trough, I feel particularly low and I sense it will be one of those days when nothing will brighten my mood. Sometimes I am able to rise above it but today my whole body has been hijacked by the toxicity of my mind and I need to manage the day more carefully than normal. Circumstances contrive to make life difficult as I am immediately one on one with my boy. He is happily munching his toast as I switch on the kettle and wait for it to boil. He has cut the bread, and the knife is lying menacingly on the granite bread board. I try to avoid its stare but it insists on looking at me as I stand chatting to him. Forcing a smile and making idle conversation I accept that I will have to remove it from view. The grotesque shape still appears in my peripheral vision and I decide to grab it by its long blade and place it in the dishwasher. Out of sight, out of mind.

My brain is already recognising the danger that the knife represents and into my mind comes the urge to prove that I don't want to harm my son. Why it comes I don't know, but it does and I must deal with it. I look at his back as he plays on a digital device of some kind whilst leaning on the breakfast bar and I feel bad about my need to go over in my head how much I love him and that I don't want to harm him. I should be OK with this by now but I'm not, and I am unable to move the knife into the machine and shut the door because that wouldn't prove anything. It would simply convince me that I can't trust myself to let it remain on the worktop, and leave me pondering what may have happened if I had.

Knowing the power of my brain I decide that today is not a good time for the challenge so I grab the long blade and walk across the room. I glance at my son as I pass and feel an awful dread in my stomach as I place the knife in the tray of the washer and quickly shut the door. I return to the kettle, feeling slightly relieved but my mind won't settle, and I wonder what would have happened if I had carried the knife by the handle, jagged blade in full view. What would have happened if I had stood behind my boy and held the knife in an aggressive way, as if prepared to draw the blade across his neck? I feel sick and disgusted with myself and all my nerves collide as I stand there knowing I have proved nothing, except perhaps to reinforce my monstrous nature.

I need to check again and this time I stand behind him. He doesn't know I am there and I urge myself to strike. I don't strike, and am able to walk away and breathe a sigh of relief. It doesn't last, and I have to test myself one more time. I pass the test but hate myself for reaching such depths of depravity. I must be the worst kind of human being.

Studying the psychiatrist's face I see no emotion, no concern or shock, he just looks back at me with hands clasped lightly in front of him and says, 'But you didn't do anything, did you?'

I replied immediately, trying to make him understand that the urge was so strong and it really felt like I wanted to kill my son. I told him that I had imagined him turning to face me at the wrong time or seeing me out of the corner of his eye, and I cried for his feelings. How would he have felt and how would I have explained myself? I remembered that it felt like I would have had to commit the horrific act.

I begged the doctor to understand how serious it was, and that on occasions, someone would walk into the room and prevent me from ticking the box. I confessed that I would wait for the next opportunity or even ask the intruder to leave to allow a further trial. I told him that I knew I loved my family dearly, above all else, and would gladly die for any one of them, but the disgust, fear and panic created by the thoughts of harm made me want to harm myself, to end it all for good. Every time I sank to the depths of despair I thought it would be impossible to sink further, but I was wrong; the chasms just became deeper and wider.

Relieved that I had done it, I knew I had told the absolute truth and now I could be sure that he knew what sort of a monster I was. I waited silently for the verdict, squeezing a small, soft hand ever more tightly.

He simply looked at me for a few moments, and calmly and quietly spoke his words of wisdom. 'Well, do you know, Oliver, I understand what you are telling me but I can assure you that people like you with such intrusive thoughts never act on their compulsions. Yes, they demonstrate ritualistic behaviours and spend long periods checking and reassuring that all is well, but as far as the awful things that you worry about go, there is absolutely no evidence that physical actions result from the thoughts.'

This statement felt too easy for my brain to comprehend and I remember hearing myself impressing upon him that sometimes it really felt like I really wanted to follow those urges, as if I was not happy being exonerated. The real truth was that I didn't want to make excuses for myself and that he needed to be absolutely clear about the real me. I repeated my admission another couple of times almost as if expecting him to suddenly react with great shock and horror and to call for a strait jacket. Of course he didn't do that; instead he left me with words that I will always remember, words that I replay when the clouds gather.

'Oliver, do you like horror stories, movies about violent serial killers and inhumane acts of aggression, those kind of gruesome movies that show blood and guts, unbelievable cruelty, brutality and terrified victims?'

'No, I hate them, I never watch them because they make me worry and concerned that I may be like some of the vilest characters. I have to be very careful what I watch, what I hear and read because all through my life I have felt so different and the most warped stories have shaped some of my greatest fears. I have suffered the simple shame of perceiving myself as the child with strange thoughts and fears all the way through to the guilt a repentant monster must face when he succumbs to the urges of his grotesque mind. I could have been a hit and run driver, a sex pest, a rapist, a mugger, wife beater, a child molester and voyeur. I could have been a murderer and torturer and even a cannibal.'

Hearing this confession, this list of potential crimes, I wondered if my judge suddenly realised he had missed something and recognised that here in front of him was someone who had finally shared his true identity. He must have at least been a little edgy and slightly suspicious. A Sikh psychiatrist allowing such a man to roam the streets must mean something, mustn't it?

I told myself that irrespective of his opinion, in my head I had done all of those things and delivered unspeakable evil, but something in me knew that in the real world I couldn't inflict pain or suffering on any living creature. A small bird mauled by our cat and too far gone to save was a step too far for me. I could barely put it out of its misery even though I tried so hard. My attempt caused me terrible guilt because I actually prolonged its agony, unable to be decisive and clinical in finishing the job. My wife had to step in.

The sick pet gerbil had to be euthanized by my youngest son because I couldn't face the thought of taking its life. I feel ashamed to admit that I cry too often, usually over the most innocuous things, silly fictional tragedies on TV, fleeting memories of times gone by and the terrible thoughts that have cursed my life. My tendency to take on board the pain and suffering of others wears me down as I am powerless to help. The temptation for me to accept I am a fraud because it cannot be real is overpowering. The two extremes, good and evil, simply don't make sense. I am a paradox or maybe a compulsive liar.

The psychiatrist didn't have to explain the meaning of his question as I recognised that he likened my thoughts to the machinations of an author seeking to pen the most shocking fantasy for his or her blood-lusting readers. He or she of all people should worry about the direction of his or her creative mind. It makes me wonder how I would have survived this long if I had a more vivid imagination. Where would I be now if my grey matter had produced *Nightmare on Elm Street* or *Kill Bill*, *The Shining* or *Silence of the Lambs*?

It was a lightbulb moment and I decided he might be right and my thoughts were normal. The abnormal aspect was the forensic analysis of every thought and action, intensified by unrealistic and unreasonable expectation. My problem was that I dwelled too long, analysed too deeply, I was overly sensitive, possibly verging on paranoid. This diagnosis failed to fill me with optimism as my defective brain chemistry remained a barrier to the truth, but at least the kind man in the orange turban had faith in me. Maybe it was time for me to have some faith in myself.

We left the clinic and I felt more positive than ever before, or was it my imagination? I wondered if this feeling would last, given my history of questioning, but I had a good feeling this time. My wife told me that she, too, could see the light at the end of the tunnel and I hoped she really believed in her vision because she deserved it to be true. That night I fell asleep after an age, not because I was stressed or in ritual mode but because I was considering turning to optimism as I moved towards my half century on this planet.

56. Full steam ahead.

That single consultation gave me the incentive to think of my life in a different way. I wanted the future to be less of a challenge and more of an adventure and I warmed to the idea that my thoughts were considered by a professional to be nothing more than the momentary flashes of imagination that everyone has from time to time.

Unless my immediate circle of friends and colleagues had been infiltrated by more than your average number of warped individuals, (whatever that figure may be) a recent impromptu and unexpected comment from one of my closest friends made me sit up and take notice. Having loosely discussed my obsessive nature on several late nights on the town over the past thirty years I thought I knew him extremely well. Without being completely transparent and keeping some of my more troubling thoughts under wraps, I was explaining that my obsession with exercise was largely for mental health and personal wellbeing purposes rather than physical benefits and that without it, my continuing existence may have been questionable. I knew he was a sensitive chap, eternal bachelor, set in his ways but a wholly decent bloke. He surprised me by a completely out of the blue confession that although he realised he didn't suffer in the same way as me, he too had experienced his fair share of strange thoughts.

This revelation aroused my interest and when I urged him to tell more, he said, 'When I was younger I used to think I wanted to murder people.' Taken aback, I asked if he meant this as a figure of speech, a response to an irritation, an annoyance or a fleeting plan for retribution. His response astounded me. 'No,' he said, 'Let's say for example I was at the railway station, I would sometimes think of pushing a stranger on to the track.'

I asked him if he had mulled over the thought for any length of time and if it had made any lasting impact on his life. The answer was an emphatic, 'No, but I did have to turn away and move in the opposite direction.' Here was a successful, middle-aged man who had briefly entertained malicious ill will towards his fellow man, the difference being that he had managed to shrug it off and move on. I promised to share my story with him in good time while I wondered if this was just a strange coincidence or a regular human instinct where obvious danger exists. Perhaps I should conduct a confidential survey just to find out how many people have stood on the platform and had to turn their back on a ghastly thought.

The psychiatrist had organised some therapy for me and, encouraged by my newfound motivation, I looked forward to learning more about the reasons for my troubles. I imagined picking up some simple coping mechanisms that would complement my own primitive tactics and enable me to deal with the bad times more easily. Could it be that a series of Cognitive Behavioural Therapy (CBT) sessions would provide a gateway to a brighter future? I imagined they had been offered rather too late for me but I understood their potential value and despite my reservations attended as advised. The early days, although a little repetitive and somewhat monotonous, armed me with some interesting coping strategies. Meticulous diary entries allowed me to build up a timeline of my mood swings, the pinch points for stress and the signs that warned me of an impending downward spiral. I was able to recognise the onset of deep depression and occasionally to anticipate an emerging peak by looking at the mood fluctuations driven by OCD, simply by the numbers recorded on my crude anxiety scale.

The whole therapy idea had been a difficult thing for me to embrace as I associated the word with my previous attempts to combat the disorder. The hypnotherapy and relaxation, and to some extent the brief encounter with religion had all failed miserably and I was sceptical of the chances of success. The acute awareness that ultimately it would be down to me and any amount of external intervention would be futile, was further fuelled by my unerring lack of trust in the establishment, in anybody for that matter.

I had needed to be independent for so long, but to my surprise the benefits gained from CBT were tangible. Sadly, the man who had opened my eyes to the enigma of harmful thoughts was unable to see me again as he had been re-assigned to look after the mental health of the elderly. The next time I saw him in the big saloon car, he didn't recognise me, he just looked away, making me realise I was just part of the job. Perhaps his indifference was a sign that he had no fears about this fearful obsessive, because if he had, a second glance would have been a certainty.

57. A chance encounter.

Time passed and the temptation to believe that I had moved on a little became more and more powerful. Family life was fulfilling, increasingly enjoyable and generally filled with lots of pleasant experiences. I was actually enjoying being a proper father and husband and although my closest allies were all aware of the bad times, they tended to accept them as part of normality, understanding their origins and accepting their impact. The children thrived in a happy environment and never once demonstrated any signs of anxiety as a result of my failings, but of course only time will tell.

They learned at a young age that mental illness is just like any other affliction and to them there is no distinction between depression and a broken leg, or OCD and a stroke. They have developed an empathy and understanding and along with their adult siblings I am sure that if they were to encounter the type of bigotry and discrimination I previously faced, they would most certainly challenge the culprits. Not just because of me but because they understand. An encounter with one of my old acquaintances proved this to me a few years ago.

Whilst carrying out Community Fire Safety visits with residents of a social housing scheme, I knocked on the door of a small maisonette, accompanied by a member of my crew. The strategy to engage with the community, fit free smoke alarms and provide advice to improve public safety was a key performance indicator for the service and we were required to complete a certain number of visits every tour of duty. Despite being cognisant of the intention and potential benefits of the activity, for many of the team it became part of the daily routine that was least pleasurable as it was seen as a box-ticking exercise. Sometimes however, mundane visits would present us with situations that required additional intervention and further engagement with local authority partners. Referrals to Social Services or the Community Health Trust to ensure that vulnerable or at risk individuals were on the radar and could be afforded a viable support network occasionally made the work more fulfilling. This visit was one such occasion.

The door opened and I was surprised to see a familiar face. Jerry had been a patient at the asylum during my stay and he recognised me immediately, despite not having set eyes on me for many years. He looked very much the same with deeply sunken eyes and the effects of sedative medication clearly visible on his face.

He remarked on remembering that I was a fireman when we were in hospital together and after initially being slightly embarrassed because of my colleagues' presence I talked to him about the past and the obvious improvement in his health since that time. He mentioned his daughter and I remembered him talking all those years ago about a baby that he had never seen.

The claim had been viewed with some scepticism by fellow patients, because the poor lad had been so heavily sedated at the time it was hard to tell if he was inventing happy families or if he genuinely had a child. He told me that he still hadn't met her but it was her birthday soon and she would be twenty one. Momentarily I thought I could see the sadness in his eyes but he immediately went on to tell me he was forty and without pausing moved on to his CD collection.

Jerry had been sectioned and admitted to the asylum as a twenty-year-old, but having undergone a couple of years of treatment and being cared for in the community he spent a further year in a retirement home as a halfway house solution. It seems that the Mental Health Trust had no other accommodation for him at the time and therefore he lived like an elderly person until the maisonette became available and he had been considered capable of being almost self-sustainable. He still had the support of the Community Mental Health System but was largely left to fend for himself.

That could be seen by the condition of his accommodation as he had surrounded himself with the clutter associated with someone seeking solace in possessions, almost to the extent of suffocating his living space. Something of a hoarder I decided. Perhaps this OCD-type trait meant we were more alike that I could have ever imagined. My immediate concern was his music CD collection, hundreds of them lining the walls, almost encasing his sleeping space, leaving no room to move and with no adequate smoke detection in the property.

We said our goodbyes to Jerry after an hour or so, having fitted a couple of smoke alarms in his little home. We helped him to free up some floor space to make sure he had a decent escape route just in case, and advised him on management of his electrical devices and his night-time routine. Leaving him grinning widely in his doorway I was thankful to be able to lead my life and to be in a position to help an old acquaintance. It was a humbling experience after which I considered myself fortunate that aside from genetics and a little luck, it might have been me at the door waving energetically at two normal people.

Questions were tactfully raised by my colleague and I talked about my first meeting with Jerry. I was quietly proud that I felt no need to make excuses or hide the shame that had once haunted me. Confidently sharing a part of my life that was long since gone, I was happy to be me; I was fortunate to be me.

Sitting at home that evening I thought again about Jerry and our first encounter in the day room at the asylum. He had been a troubled individual, throwing himself to the floor, playing dead for no apparent reason. I had initially been concerned but was told by nursing staff to move away and leave him to it. They could not or would not explain why he acted in this way, so as far as the patients were concerned, it was just Jerry behaving as Jerry did.

He had regularly been left to stew in his own juices until discreetly raising his head to see if anyone was watching. Then he would shuffle off to his bed, without a word, looking bereft that no one had been taken in by his performance. Some days he could be a happy and talkative chap, his conversation usually limited to his childhood, the fabled baby and the odd attempt at a juvenile joke. Nothing ever made much sense but I suspect the drugs had somehow switched off his brain.

The day before I had left the ward, the familiar sound of the siren had blasted around the building, indicating that someone had absconded, someone unlike me, not free to come and go as they pleased. Sounding like an old Second World War air raid warning, everyone had been intrigued and, like excited youngsters, couldn't wait to discover what had happened.

I'd wondered if the horrendous alarm had endured since the 1940s or if it had been installed following the terrible fire in the 1960s, when some twenty one of the eight hundred patients had died, most of them as they lay asleep in their beds. One of my old bosses, a firefighter on that fateful day, described a dreadful scene. He recalled that many of the victims had been under lock and key and would have stood little chance of escape, even if they had been awake. Perhaps my experience of the asylum wasn't so bad after all.

It had turned out that Jerry had done a runner and a frantic search had been undertaken involving hospital staff, the police helicopter and local constabulary. It had materialised that it wasn't exactly a surprise, as the poor lad apparently had a penchant for disappearing if given the slightest opportunity, but at least that had given the chasing posse an idea of some of his usual haunts.

Suffice to say, within about three hours of being reported missing he had been spotted at the nearby Accident and Emergency hospital, half a mile from where we eagerly awaited news. He had been discovered parading around one of the medical wards wearing a white coat and sporting a stethoscope around his neck. He had made an awful fuss as he was persuaded to return the fancy dress to the staff room and return to the asylum, but it had made the day more interesting for fellow patients who, despite their own problems, enjoyed his antics and considered him quite a character.

Feeling pleased that he had made it to the outside world, following our first encounter in mainstream society I began to bump into him quite regularly. He would tell me how he was feeling and that his regular dose of intravenous medication kept him calm and on the straight and narrow.

My youngest child met him too, and she was keen to know the history behind our friendship, reacting maturely when I told her that we had been in hospital together many years before. She was ten years old and remarked that he looked very tired and glum but had a kind face and said funny things. I explained that his medication made him appear that way because he had some serious mental health issues that required regular injections and he needed lots of support.

She was confused that he seemed different and also struggled with the concept that we were in hospital together when I acted like a normal person and he didn't. I explained to her that mental illness in its many different guises, often invisible to the rest of the world, was much the same as those we are able to see and deserved an equal amount of respect and understanding. That was enough for her on the face of it, but despite my openness about my own problems, I could see that she found it hard to accept that Jerry and I were very similar.

Personally, I was thrilled that a man with very little and whom everyone had written off, was able to function in the real world. He would always wave when he saw me driving past in my car wearing my uniform, considering me his fireman friend and he didn't miss an opportunity to tell people we had shared a hospital ward.

Sadly, however, during the last year or so when our paths have crossed, he seems to have forgotten me completely. Now I merely see an empty shell, a sad, vacant expression on his face, his forehead deeply lined and sagging cheeks ageing him way beyond his years. I smile at him as he shuffles past, puffing on his cigarette. His lack of response must be down to the medication but I hope our next encounter will be more satisfying and he will have recovered that vital spark of recognition that will tell me he is living and not just surviving.

58. A different perspective.

The unconcerned psychiatrist had previously set a review date for me to attend the clinic to meet his replacement. For once I was seriously looking forward to speaking with a mental health professional and had no preconceptions or worries about the reaction I would face. Finally, after so many years of battling with myself I felt the need to share what I considered to be a certain amount of success. I was still in the woods but there were clear signs that the canopy was getting thinner, allowing some little rays of sunshine to poke their way through.

Supported by my faithful ally, I walked into the stark office to see a rotund man facing me, peering over his wire-rimmed spectacles. There was no hint of a smile as he welcomed us and waved his hand towards some chairs, motioning us to take a seat. Funny how you make judgments about people way too early, and can't quite put your finger on how you came to that conclusion. This was one such occasion.

Sometimes it's just a feeling and although many of us like to think we are intuitive and have the ability to judge character within the first few minutes, more often than not we are wrong. This man was nothing like my previous psychiatrists, he had no gentle demeanour, he had an adversity to smiling and wasn't particularly hot on listening, appearing to be somewhat distracted. I decided immediately that this would be our first and last encounter and that I wouldn't need a second opinion, my gut reaction providing me with sufficient information to end our relationship as soon as it had begun.

He wanted me to give him an outline of my history in relation to OCD and he nodded as I explained how the illness, combined with severe bouts of depression had ruled my life for decades. Without detailing the finer points, the more harrowing episodes, it must have sounded like nothing more than the ramblings of some immature adolescent who spent his life playing video games, immersed in a world of fantasy. I explained that the Sikh psychiatrist before him had made great strides in reassuring me with his observations and since then, although recognising my illness was part of me and always would be, I had come to terms with its peculiarities.

I was able to recognise my mood and reduce distress by managing exposure to certain trigger points. I told him that I worked hard to avoid suicidal thoughts as I had discovered that the more credence I allowed them, the more I tended to slide into despair. I admitted that I knew the futility of it all and that the rituals and compulsions were simply a way of reassuring me that I had done enough. I also admitted that on reflection I always knew that the outcomes I imagined were largely inconceivable but I was unable to stop the rituals because it would mean that I had not protected, not cared enough to act, or not taken adequate precautions.

Leaving myself vulnerable to criticism and ridicule I owned up to the fact that I knew my whole life had been a journey of make-believe. I forgot to tell him that I had no control over the direction of that journey, and that it had taken me over forty years to reach this destination. I should have explained to him that my brain makes me behave irrationally by constantly evaluating everything on the basis of worst case scenario.

He finally entered the discussion and I almost wish that he had remained in nodding mode for the entire consultation. He passed his opinions on my naïve understanding of OCD and depression and how I had worked out the link between the two. His direct approach was slightly unnerving and straight away I got the feeling that he had no time for people who were unable to see what was in front of their nose. As far as he was concerned the pain and suffering I had endured for most of my life was no more than a childish excuse to ignore reality.

I couldn't help feeling hurt by his diagnosis and the manner in which it was delivered, particularly as it was the introduction of a whole new concept for my brain to accept. His words bore no sensitivity and immediately set my mind racing, wondering if he was the only person who had called it correctly and all the pleasant advice and support I had benefitted from in previous years had been designed only to make me feel better and perhaps to prevent further suicidal tendencies.

My wife and I looked at each other and she smiled, but she could see the hurt in my face and grabbed my hand, squeezing it tightly. The man in front of me, his blank eyes appearing to look at me but failing to see, forced a smile as I thanked him for his time. Driving home in silence I made a promise to myself that I wouldn't let this brief encounter destroy the progress we had made together. Knowing the promise would be hard to keep, I was determined that this day would not be remembered for signalling the beginning of another downward spiral.

59. Food for thought.

Following this blunt appraisal, I couldn't help but start to analyse my past and all the things that had created so many bad memories over the years. I started by thinking about the early days and my first encounter with damaging thoughts and urges, the time I sensed danger for Mum, but eventually scared myself half to death by deducing that it was more a desire than a fear. That of course could be considered a childish and immature reaction from a small boy battling with his insecurity and a blatant lack of parental understanding. The fact that today I suffer this legacy from childhood may well imply that I have simply failed to grow up.

Strangely, whilst walking in the street I assume that I both feel and look just like everyone else despite the battles going on in my head. Sometimes the battles are minor skirmishes and more often than not these days they are just thoughts that barely scratch the surface.

I would hate to think that I am seen as a constant victim because I am now beginning to believe in myself. My periods of sadness and misery seem to be decreasing as I learn to function like the rest of the world. My only concern is that when people see me as a regular, stand-up type of chap, they are unaware of my past and what if they were able to get under my skin, see inside my brain and observe the real me? They may see that I am not the man I claim to be, the man who functions normally, if normal is my aspiration. Anyway, what is normal? To some it may be me.

I remember mentioning to the nice psychiatrist that my intrusive thoughts have been so extreme that on a bad day I could have convinced myself I was guilty of the most horrific acts.

Having never been caught on the wrong side of the law I can't help wondering if 'thoughts maketh the man'. I start to think about one of life's most emotive and distressing subjects and can't help feeling upset. I heard of an individual, who like me had not committed a crime, but had exposed himself as a paedophile in mind although not in actions. Whilst he confessed that his brain was wired in such a way that his sexual urges leaned towards the molestation of children, on no occasion had he carried out his fantasies, nor did he intend to succumb to his urges.

Knowing very little about the context of his revelation I am staggered that he elected to put himself in the spotlight in such an extreme way. My assumption is that his admission was in some way an attempt to appeal for compassion and understanding because he had been born with a brain that through no fault of his own was wired a certain way and he had fought against it, battling to remain vaguely human.

Listening to a radio programme debating the issue, there was some support for his bravery and honesty whilst many contributors displayed the type of vitriol usually reserved for convicted offenders. We all know how easy it is to fall into the trap of prematurely assuming guilt but I was surprised that many callers considered him to be no better than the worst serial offender. I don't want to argue the case for or against the morality of his decision or the way in which we should assess his threat to society but I have to admit that it raises questions about my own credibility.

The experts don't see me as a danger in any way, but what concerns me is how I perceive myself. This alternative way of looking at the meaning of my most devastating thoughts has definitely given me food for thought.

With my confidence threatening to desert me, I have decided that I at least will accept my innocence for the time being and ignore the mountain of negativity my mind is trying to impose. It has taken a long time but at last I feel I may be in a position to manage my emotional brain by allowing some form of rational human influence to take over. Failing that, I know I can always consider myself a child and continue along the well-trodden path of righteous immaturity.

The idea of fighting harder appeals to me more than giving up and accepting defeat as I know only too well that my depression thrives on the kind of negativity that generates the thoughts of taking my own life. Such thoughts never improve things for me, they drag me down further, so I resolve to avoid the temptation and to accept that I have too much to live for these days. I have already left it far too long.

60. Temptation.

Trying to turn my back on a lifetime of irrational thinking is more difficult than I could ever have imagined. The craving for continuous reassurance never goes away and the urge to test and retest to demonstrate the purity of my thoughts and of honourable intentions is rarely far from my mind.

The intensity of the urge to put myself close to the edge of the plateau is immense and propensity to confuse fears with desires is still my biggest challenge. The difference now is that I see this crazy mentality as exactly that, a crazy mentality that I am challenged to overcome. When I begin to dwell on a situation that threatens irrational thoughts, I focus on the positives. I remind myself that it usually starts with just a feeling or a sense of foreboding with no tangible cause, a hair trigger pulled by a momentary flash of light in my brain.

I remind myself that without exception the fear of harming others grows from a series of repetitive thoughts that reflect my need to protect. The presence of a weapon such as a knife or a hammer and the harm it may cause, raises no more fear than say, a dinner plate or a tea towel, because each can morph into a lethal weapon. It is my brain and the image it provokes that creates the anxiety.

Where head-on exposure to most forms of obsessional behaviour and the introduction of coping strategies is often the key to managing the illness, I know that for me sometimes the opposite is true. My greatest compulsions have to be avoided unless I am entirely sure that the spectre of doubt has been banished from my brain. I am not advocating this as a one size fits all, but personally I find it far less distressing, far less frightening and more importantly it works for me!

Whilst still occasionally picking myself up from the odd stumble, I am learning to trust my instincts and walk away from any form of negative temptation. At last I now have the strength and knowledge to accept my obsessions and rituals, my intrusive thoughts and unfulfilled urges and impulses for what they really are: abnormal and extreme reactions to normal, everyday brain activity.

Because my working life has changed so much over recent years many of the higher risk activities have been removed and when I do feel less able to cope, the opportunities for my mind to dwell on escaping my pain have diminished. What I mean is that as a member of a fire crew I was regularly exposed to the hazards associated with fast flowing water, toxic chemicals, fire and smoke and rescues from height, a bridge, a tree or a multi-storey building. During the worst times these could provide instant suicide opportunities.

With newfound determination and increased understanding of my condition I avoid such pitfalls because I realise now that the more I saw my own death as a means of protecting others, the more it became ingrained. The depression would deepen, perpetuating the cycle and further reducing my resolve. The thought that I could disguise my death as an accident and allow my family financial security and eternal safety, was a real temptation and something that only now I am able to share. The truth is that in the past I was never quite sure when I may have needed to opt out completely.

Many years ago on a beautifully sunny day I was climbing up the old turntable ladder and as I ascended I felt sick with depression. The ladder was pitched in an almost vertical position as this meant it could be extended to its maximum of one hundred feet. Wearing a very basic waist harness belt I reached the top and secured my position by attaching the clip on the harness to the metal ring at the head of the ladder.

Confirming this to the turret operator via the in-built loudspeaker I commenced my fairground ride above the drill yard. Normally a unique and stimulating experience and one that very few people ever have the opportunity to enjoy, I focused on my mood rather than the panoramic view over the rooftops. Thinking of my demise instead of surveying the extent of the town and perhaps counting the church spires I concentrated on the small ring securing me to the ladder. The wind rushed past my helmet as the ladder rotated full circle and I reached to my right and released the clip.

My legs felt weaker in reaction to the freedom of movement and imminent danger and I imagined myself crashing to the floor with colleagues standing around me in shock. Would the helmet protect me and allow me to survive or would the authorities be aware of my history and surmise that my death was no accident and refuse to pay out? How had the clip become detached from the ring? It would be just my luck to become a broken burden for my family for the rest of my life. Frightened, confused and ashamed I clipped back in, deciding that the plan had to be foolproof and must not result in any kind of stigma for those left behind.

I didn't feel proud of myself for fighting the urge, but I recall how easy it could have been to take the plunge. The strange thing is that for as long as I can remember I have dreamt of being able to fly like a bird of prey. I see myself lift off the ground with a fluttering action rather like treading water. Once in the air I accelerate to phenomenal speeds, swooping and diving at low level, whilst everyone on the ground gasps in amazement, awestruck at my superhuman ability.

I don't think the dream has ever filled me with delusions of invincibility or the craving for adoring followers to consider me their idol, but there has to be an underlying reason. The psychologists say that repetitive dreams have certain meanings depending on the circumstances and the personality of the dreamer but I doubt mine has anything to do with having a successful and controlled flight back to terra firma. My dreams are always so realistic that I like to think they signal my desire and intention to make the most of my life and maybe to fly in the face of adversity.

Years later, my Watch visited the market hall clock standing proud at the centre of the town. A group of us climbed the internal ladder to explore and get acquainted with the internal layout of the tower and any inherent risks. We all emerged from the small door leading on to the sloping roof some eighty feet above surrounding buildings. I am not overly brave and quite frankly can take or leave heights but I just had to force myself to stand right at the edge of the shallow pitch and contemplate the quickest way down.

The worrying thing at the time was that I wasn't feeling particularly low, had not been building up to this moment for any particular reason; I simply had an incredible urge to jump. I have heard there is a strange phenomenon that inspires people to do this when they stand on the edge of a ravine, a cliff edge or a tall building, even though they may have no apparent death wish. I wondered if this was one occasion where mine was a normal thought and if anyone else had cared to join me, they too would have felt the same.

No one else went to the edge. They just agreed I was crazy to stand there. If only they knew. There have been so many other occasions over the years when circumstances have provided me with the opportunity to remove myself from the life I had learned to detest, but somehow I resisted the temptation. Perhaps it was a childish game inside my head.

The fact that I have managed to come to terms with the past and believe there is a future is a major victory for me but I cannot help wondering if these repeated moments of weakness are a clear sign of my immaturity and inability to grow up. After all, how many opportunities does one need to commit suicide? One thing I can say for sure is that it was not a cry for help. I am certain of that because I have never uttered a word, nor did I intend to, but if my survival is an indication that there is hope for anyone, being labelled a child is a burden I am happy to carry.

61 Happy being me.

Finally I recognise who I really am and although like most people, I thrive on being liked and being considered a good person, the craving for acceptance and to conform to the opinions of my peers no longer ranks so highly on my scale of social needs. Within the last ten years, particularly in the workplace, I have observed a definite change in mood in terms of how mental illness is viewed by non-specialists. What I mean is that those employed to deal with personnel, the human resource and wider management fraternity have always needed to comply with standard equality and diversity issues.

On the other hand, there remained an underlying culture of intolerance on the shop floor. Not so much today though, but perhaps I only notice this because I have changed my approach in recent years and my previous overwhelming desire to hide my failings from prying eyes and ears has fallen by the wayside. My participation in secretive, obsessional toilet breaks and hygiene rituals has been replaced by frank admission to various aspects of the illness, and extends to sharing some of the less disturbing compulsions. No one in their right mind would own up to the heavy stuff, but the less sinister obsessions, popularised by mainstream TV, seemed an obvious place to start.

Comments from people who seem to know a little about the illness have become more and more frequent and this makes the conversation more comfortable. My explanation that the condition is genetic, hard wired, and that I have no choice but to face it every single day seems to hit home.

I often mention the statistics and that one in four people will suffer from some form of mental illness during their lifetime and that we as a service witness more and more stress-related illnesses. Some consider these disorders as the twenty-first-century back injury. This is a reference to a long gone Fire Service tradition where personnel would be able to wangle a full-pension early retirement based on the once infallible dodgy back syndrome. I doubt that history will repeat itself with this modern day epidemic.

Strangely, the terminology used to describe such absences still bears echoes of the stigma I found so deep seated in the old days. We call it 'stress related' because it sounds more user friendly. I am familiar with cases where genuine mental health issues exist in the service and occasionally the level of tolerance and compassion from colleagues leaves a lot to be desired but then I guess some people simply refuse to change. However, with increased exposure to mental illness, health professionals and the man in the street have the power to reduce institutional and societal ignorance to an acceptable level, if not to eradicate it completely.

The construction of modern, bright, apartment-like accommodation for the mentally ill, indistinguishable from, and often sharing the same site as, mainstream medical and surgical facilities is an important step forward. More importantly perhaps, the Victorian asylum is largely a thing of the past. Sadly, underfunding and a lack of proper facilities in which to treat the mentally ill means that many sufferers, including juveniles, are forced to be accommodated in police cells until beds become available. Certainly not something you would expect in the twenty-first century.

Epilogue.

My life is ahead of me now and strange as it may sound at the age of fifty three, I genuinely feel excited about the future. If I should have any regrets at all about my passage from childhood to late middle age it would be that I failed to get help at an early stage. Too many years were wasted through a combination of ignorance, fear and lethargy, and with the benefit of hindsight and experience as a father, the negative impact of a dysfunctional family unit.

The brain is a powerful machine but at the same time extremely sensitive to neglect. Weakness given time to develop during those important formative years is likely to come back to haunt you. The hard wiring, the blueprint, may already be in place and the nature predisposed but the value of early intervention, constant support and a means of compensating for that chemical deficiency cannot be underestimated.

The secret formula for success is simple. I call it my five Ss: Sport, Sunlight, Support, Stimulation and Serotonin. Without these vital components I know I wouldn't be here today to tell my story.

To put this into context I recently suffered a blip in my recovery. Revelling in a prolonged spell of good times, I failed to remember the depths to which I could sink and because the signs of a decline in mood escaped me, I fell into a deep depression. Circumstances and naivety contrived to exacerbate the process by denying me most of my coping mechanisms. The winter months are always the worst and the sunlight that normally improves my wellbeing was long gone. Exercise was halted by a serious injury and being temporarily away from home on a residential course had removed my usual support structure. To cap it all, I forgot to stay busy and had nothing to stimulate my overactive brain. My new GP soon helped to rekindle my faith in the future and although she didn't have all the answers, with the help and support of my family I was reunited with my personal cocktail for happiness and survival.

The way I am is not my fault but now long in the tooth, I am sensible enough to understand that the buck stops with me if I fail to make the most of this opportunity to enjoy the rest of my days. Though a little concerned about the effects of thirty years of medication, wondering if consumption beyond clinical trial limits will cause bits to drop off or encourage my internal organs to shut down, I can accept accountability for my destiny. I consider my journey through many trials and tribulations and the signs of a little light at the end of this long, dark tunnel as a success story in the making. Rapidly approaching the end of my career, I finally feel that I have achieved something of which I can be proud.

Twice a year I am the master of ceremonies for events celebrating the careers and achievements of my Fire Service colleagues. Presenting to between two and three hundred people I am often complimented on my calm, confident and controlled delivery. The truth is that I dread these occasions because I fear my public persona will give away the real me. This modern day challenge has me battling my inner insecurities and that fight defines my life story.

I may not be quite the majestic swan but perhaps the ugly duckling who paddles frantically below the surface in an attempt to remain afloat. My feeling since childhood of being remote from the rest of society, always looking in at myself and analysing every thought and action remains a powerful reminder that I am still the same person today, but today I understand what I am seeing.

I went to a funeral recently and during the eulogy, a lifelong friend uttered the words penned initially by a Brazilian writer named Fernando Sabino. This quote has been rewritten many times since in a variety of forms and it continues to inspire me. It says, *In the end everything will be OK. If it's not OK, it's not yet the end.*

I have learned that in life we all suffer in ways unknown to others, often the closest to us, but I have also learned to work hard at life, to expect the unexpected and count any blessings, even if they do appear insignificant. The world doesn't have to be forever black and as long as a chink of light shines through, the colours will return one day.

I am Oliver and I was born with a defective brain, but I dared to want more from life. More is what I intend to get.

The proud and decent man now stands in his rightful place,
The lengthy trail of suffering etched deeply on his face.
The lines a true reflection of a life defined by dread,
But now a sense of freedom, in his heart and in his head.

Never will he fail again to fight for all he's worth,

His strength enhanced forever with those natural gifts from birth,
Regretting nothing of his past he swears to rise again,
Emerging from the ashes like the phoenix, but from pain.

The future holds no fear for him, his conscience clear as day,
His life will never be the same, no more he'll need to pray.
But when the end comes to his life he'll know he fought the fight,
Because he passed the test of life and journeyed to the light.

2015

Acknowledgements

Huge thanks to my lovely wife and best friend, Jo, and my wonderful kids: Jenna, Scott, Ross, Jay and Molly for standing by me throughout, despite my challenging behaviour. Thanks to Deb Price and Laura and Nige Merchant for reading and advising at different stages and to my Jo for proofreading every five minutes and having the patience to keep offering a different perspective when I felt negative. I am grateful to my training partner Ian Turner for giving his honest opinion and for each one of them for encouraging me to continue after numerous publishing rejections and periods of indifference. I owe a debt of gratitude to them all and if *Ordinary Childhood Dreams* reaches out and inspires a few fellow sufferers then their contribution is proved all the more invaluable.

Fight hard to beat the curse, nothing is inevitable.

oliverrayknell@btinternet.com

References

Prof Steve Peters (2012), *The Chimp Paradox: The Mind Management Programme to Help You Achieve Success, Confidence and Happiness,* Vermilion, London.

http://thetimechamber.co.uk/beta/sites/asylums/asylum-history/the-history-of-the-asylum
http://www.healthline.com/health/depression/genetic#OtherFactors3
http://www.netdoctor.co.uk/conditions/depression/
http://www.theguardian.com/books/2014/apr/16/man-who-couldnt-stop-ocd-david-adam-review
http://www.writing-world.com/publish/bookprop1.shtml
https://www.skillsforjustice-nosfinder.com/nos/doc/EFSM2..doc
www.dailymail.co.uk/home/books/article.../Bedlam-brutal-truth.html

16028952R00157

Printed in Great Britain
by Amazon